The Squadron Diaries

Nayna Yadav

Vitasta
LET KNOWLEDGE SPREAD

Published by
Renu Kaul Verma
Vitasta Publishing Pvt Ltd
2/15, Ansari Road, Daryaganj
New Delhi - 110 002
info@vitastapublishing.com

ISBN 978-93-86473-56-1

First Edition 2019

MRP 495
Printed by Nutech Print Services - India

ACKNOWLEDGEMENT

This book would not have been possible without a great deal of help from the coolest bunch of people I have ever met. Thank you veterans of the 51st Squadron, for the stories, for protecting the borders and for just being so awesome. I extend this thanks further to other IAF pilots who helped me with this project and to all the others whose stories we do not yet know, to those who serve, to those who served and to those who are no longer with us.
Thank you all.

A big thanks to Dad for his stories, his enthusiasm and for just basically making The Squadron Diaries happen.

Thank you to Tony uncle for his time and kindness.
There can be no better Air Chief anywhere.

I thank my guide, Professor Mandar Rane for his insights and his valuable inputs and I thank IDC IIT Bombay for the opportunity to work on this project.

PREFACE

A fighter jet is the acme of advanced technology. It's a machine designed to function under unpredictable circumstances, with unknown variables and with active opposition aiming to destroy its mission. The machine by itself, however, cannot accomplish anything. The vocation of a fighter pilot is a very specialised one. At present there are probably not more than 20,000 active fighter pilots in the world. Today India has maybe less than a thousand active fighter pilots in service. The demanding nature of this profession attracts a select few and accepts fewer still.

Very few people have the privilege of being intimately familiar with the life of a IAF fighter pilot. Literature available on these aviators falls largely into two categories, the memoirs and strategy books written by high ranking officials or the authored war stories of their heroic adventures and bravery in combat.
Through this book I will attempt to create a picture of the everyday lives of these heroes. To show more than the bravado and the wars. This is a book about their stories of training, camaraderie, about fears and motivations, and most importantly, it's about them and their love of flying.

Established in 1932 under the British, The Royal Indian Air Force had the prefix Royal removed in 1950 and became Indian Air Force. Today, it ranks as the fourth largest Air Force in the world. However, according to a report by *The Hindu* in 2016, the IAF is weaker than the numbers suggested, and "At nominally 36.5 squadrons, it is well short of its sanctioned strength, and many of its frontline aircraft are obsolete."
Another report by NDTV in 2016 shared that the Indian Air Force has just 32 squadrons of fighters which is the lowest in a decade. This was confirmed to NDTV by top IAF commanders.

The IAF needs at least 42 squadrons of fighters to protect its borders. We are short of both planes and pilots. The Diplomat in 2015 shared a report by the Indian government's Standing Committee on Defence which predicts the number of squadrons may decline further yet. "With regard to this, representatives of Air Force deposed before the committee that a drawdown has already begun and, by 2022, air force will have around just 25 squadrons, thereby losing even the slight edge over rival neighboring nation". According to *The Diplomat*, the IAF's current fighter aircraft to pilot ratio is 1:0.81. This is far less than the authorized figure of 1:1.25. Pakistan Air Force's fighter to pilot ratio is 1:2.5. In the U.S. this ratio is 1:2.

There is good news too. The government has contracted for 36 French Rafale jets. Efforts are on to build up to 42 squadrons by 2027. Since 2016, the IAF has begun accepting women in the fighter stream. We now have female fighter pilots. There has been advertising in theaters, they've put up hoardings encouraging people to join the IAF. Certainly, bravery, valour and service to your country are good reasons to join the Air Force but one could join the Army, the Navy, and there are a number of other ways to serve the country. What's so great about the Air Force? It's dangerous, the pay is nothing exceptional, why do those who join it, do so? What is it really like?

Having grown up hearing first-hand accounts of fighter flying on air force bases all over the country, I find myself in a position where I have a unique perspective to offer on IAF fighter flying.

What started as a project in IIT Bombay is now going to be my first published book and through it I hope to share stories of the exhilarating, fulfilling and sometimes dangerous lives that Indian fighter pilots lead. I hope to do this in a manner that allows everyone to understand how unique an experience it is to fly a fighter jet and how addictive it is for those who do it.

The Squadron Diaries

CONTENT

NATIONAL DEFENCE ACADEMY

THE JOURNEY BEGINS

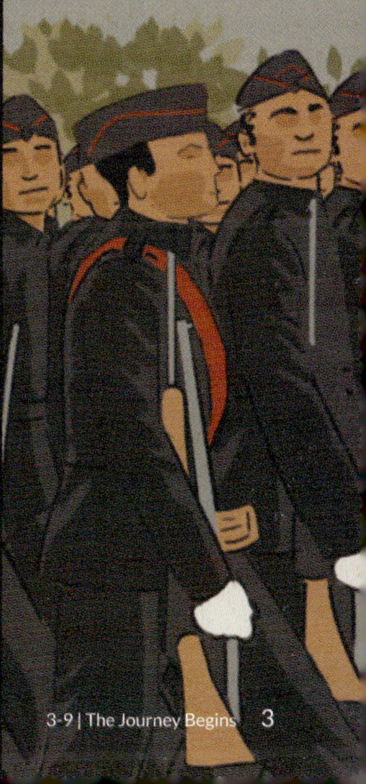

NDA

National Defence Academy. This is where the youngsters fresh out of school come to become fighter pilots in the Indian Air Force or to join other branches of the Indian military. People also join the IAF through other routes but many of the pilots whose stories have been shared here went to NDA.

NDA... That beautiful campus, those lush green lawns, that gorgeous lake... and there's gliding, parasailing, horse riding! Who wouldn't want to be there right?

So, what is NDA like?

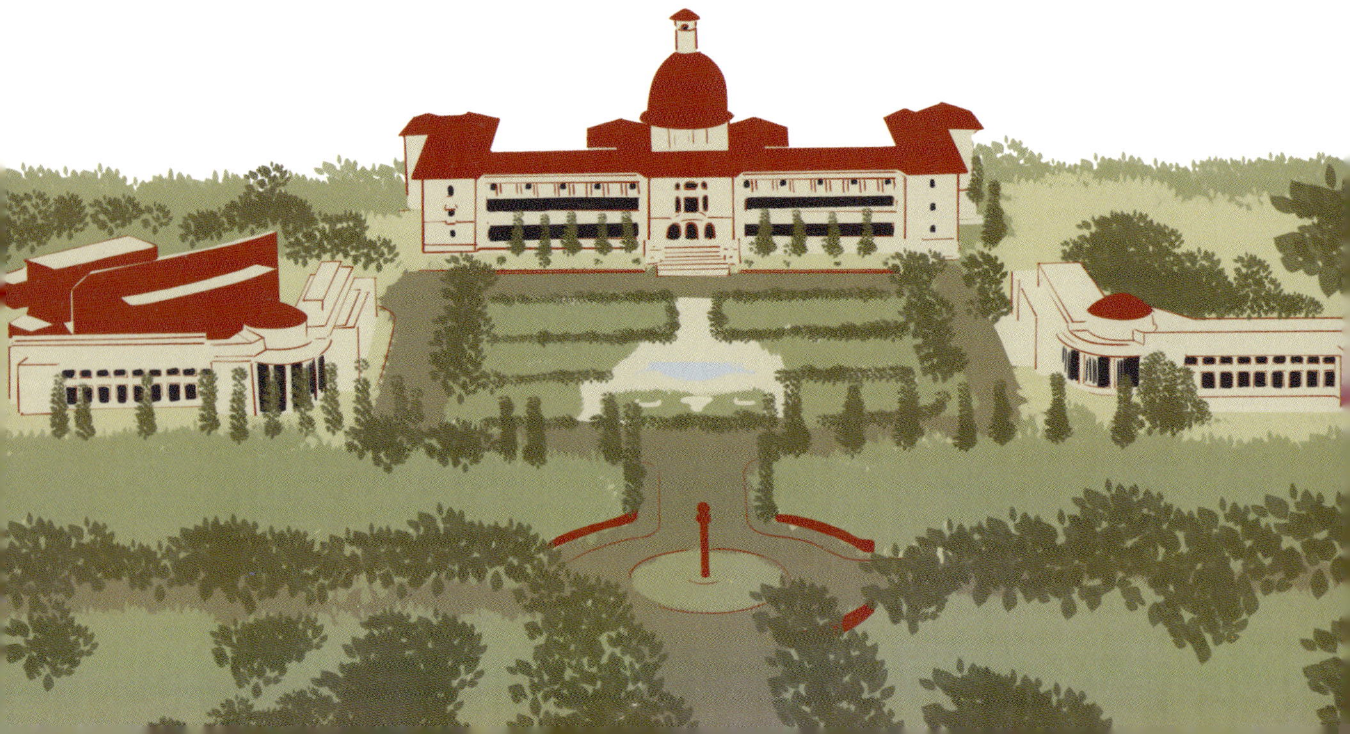

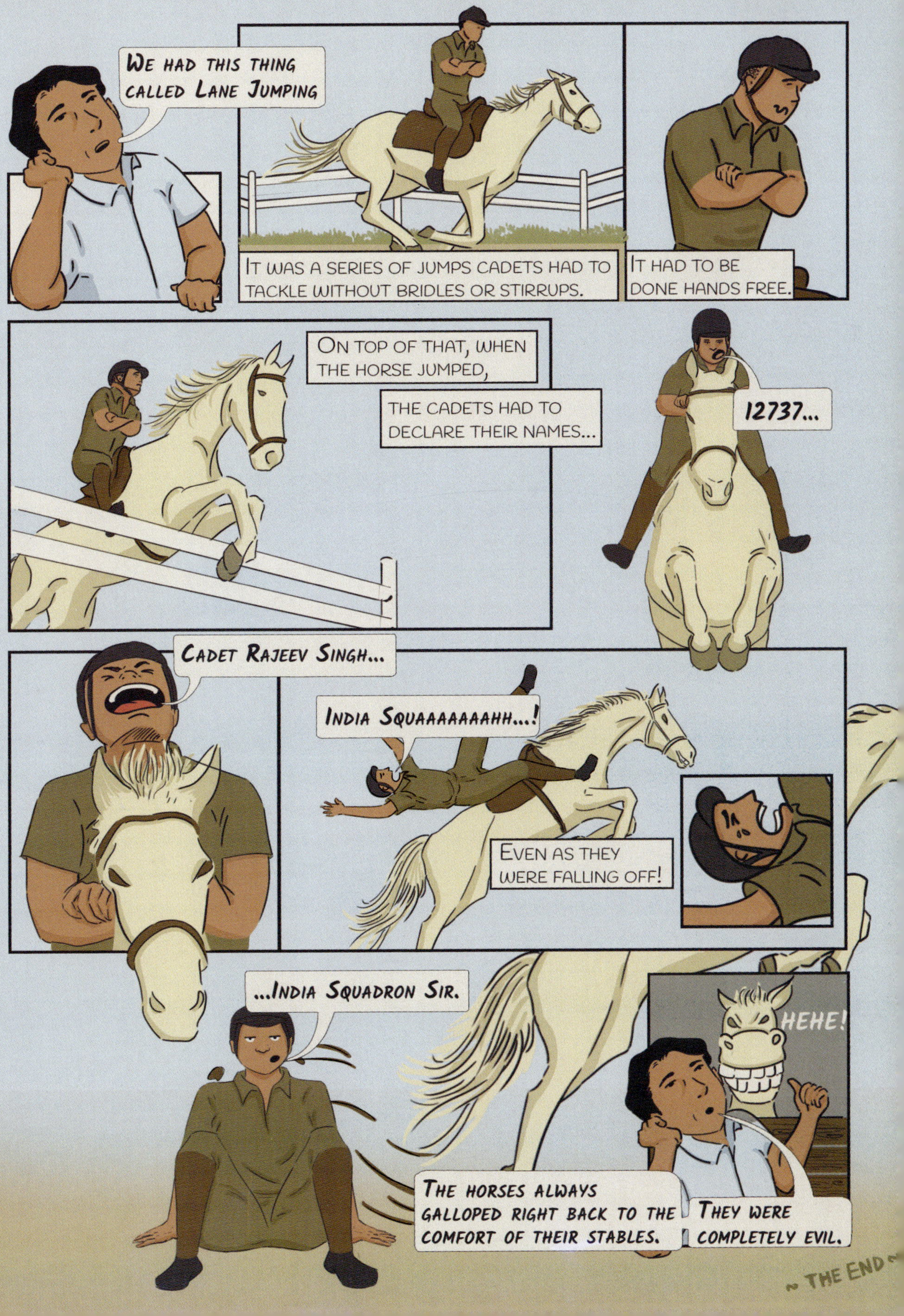
WE HAD THIS THING CALLED LANE JUMPING
IT WAS A SERIES OF JUMPS CADETS HAD TO TACKLE WITHOUT BRIDLES OR STIRRUPS.
IT HAD TO BE DONE HANDS FREE.
ON TOP OF THAT, WHEN THE HORSE JUMPED,
THE CADETS HAD TO DECLARE THEIR NAMES...
12737...
CADET RAJEEV SINGH...
INDIA SQUAAAAAAAHH...!
EVEN AS THEY WERE FALLING OFF!
...INDIA SQUADRON SIR.
HEHE!
THE HORSES ALWAYS GALLOPED RIGHT BACK TO THE COMFORT OF THEIR STABLES.
THEY WERE COMPLETELY EVIL.
~ THE END ~

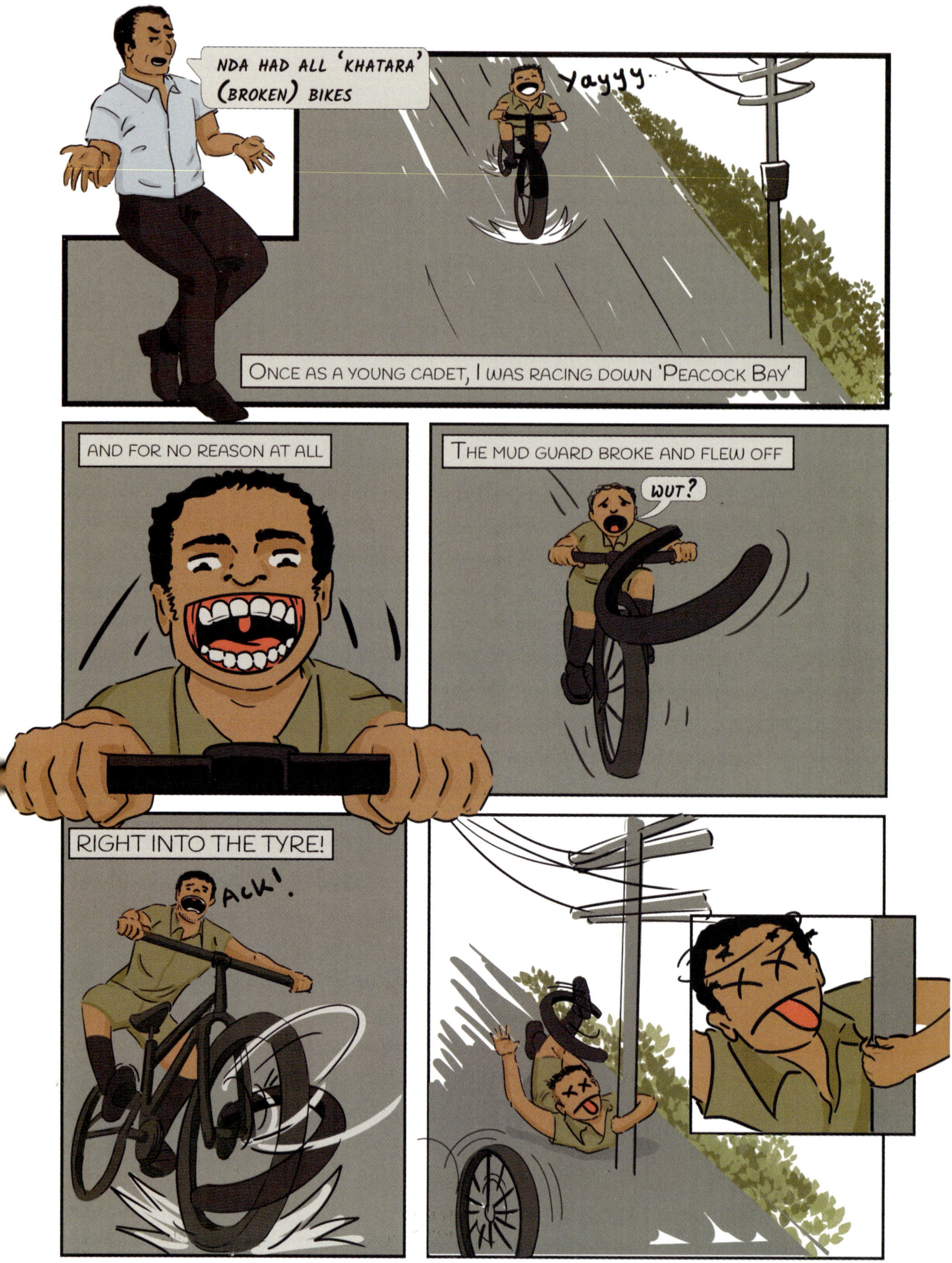
NDA HAD ALL 'KHATARA' (BROKEN) BIKES
Yayyy...
ONCE AS A YOUNG CADET, I WAS RACING DOWN 'PEACOCK BAY'
AND FOR NO REASON AT ALL
THE MUD GUARD BROKE AND FLEW OFF
WUT?
RIGHT INTO THE TYRE!
ACK!

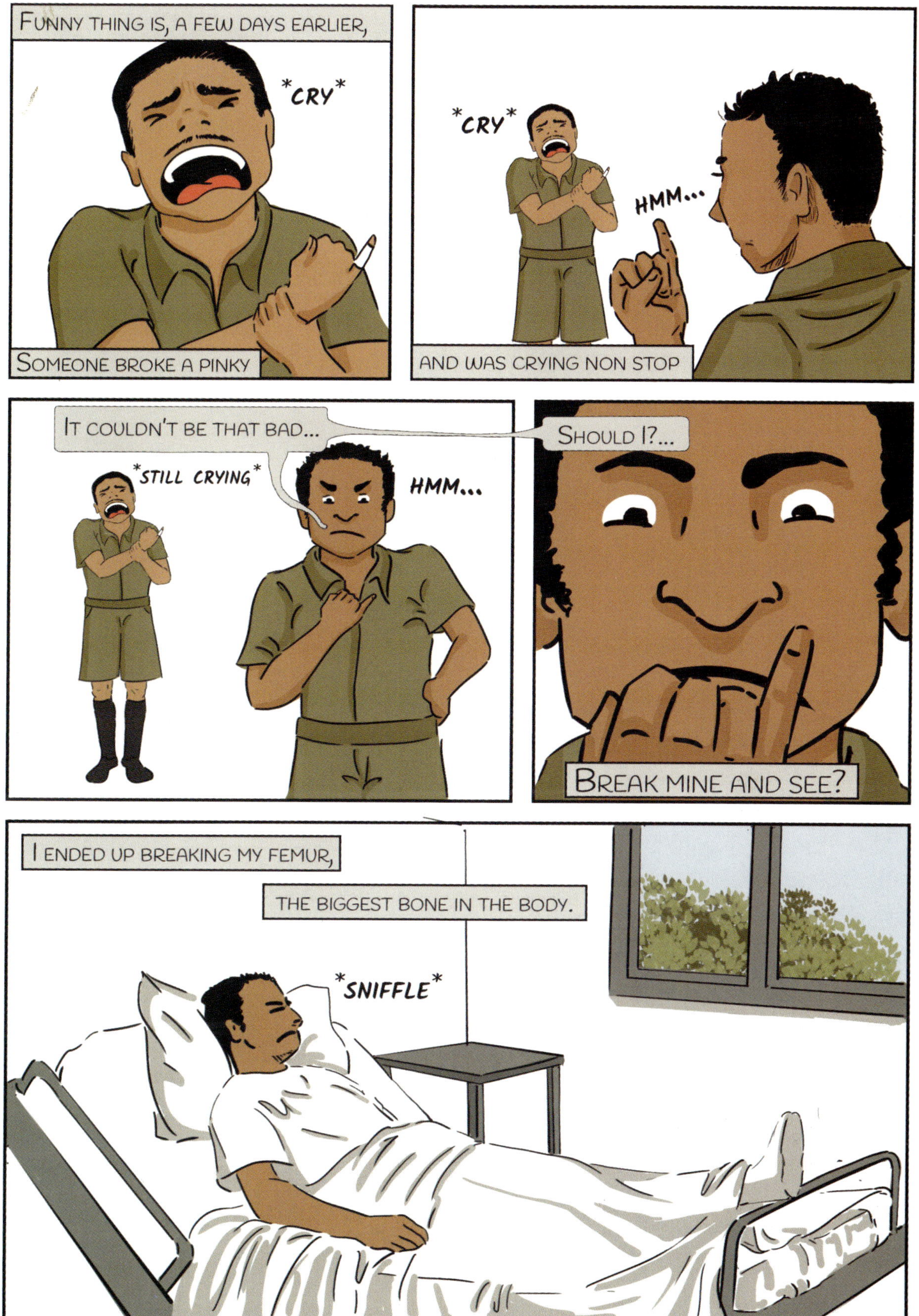
Funny thing is, a few days earlier,
CRY
Someone broke a pinky
CRY
HMM...
And was crying non stop
It couldn't be that bad...
STILL CRYING
HMM...
Should I?...
Break mine and see?
I ended up breaking my femur,
the biggest bone in the body.
SNIFFLE

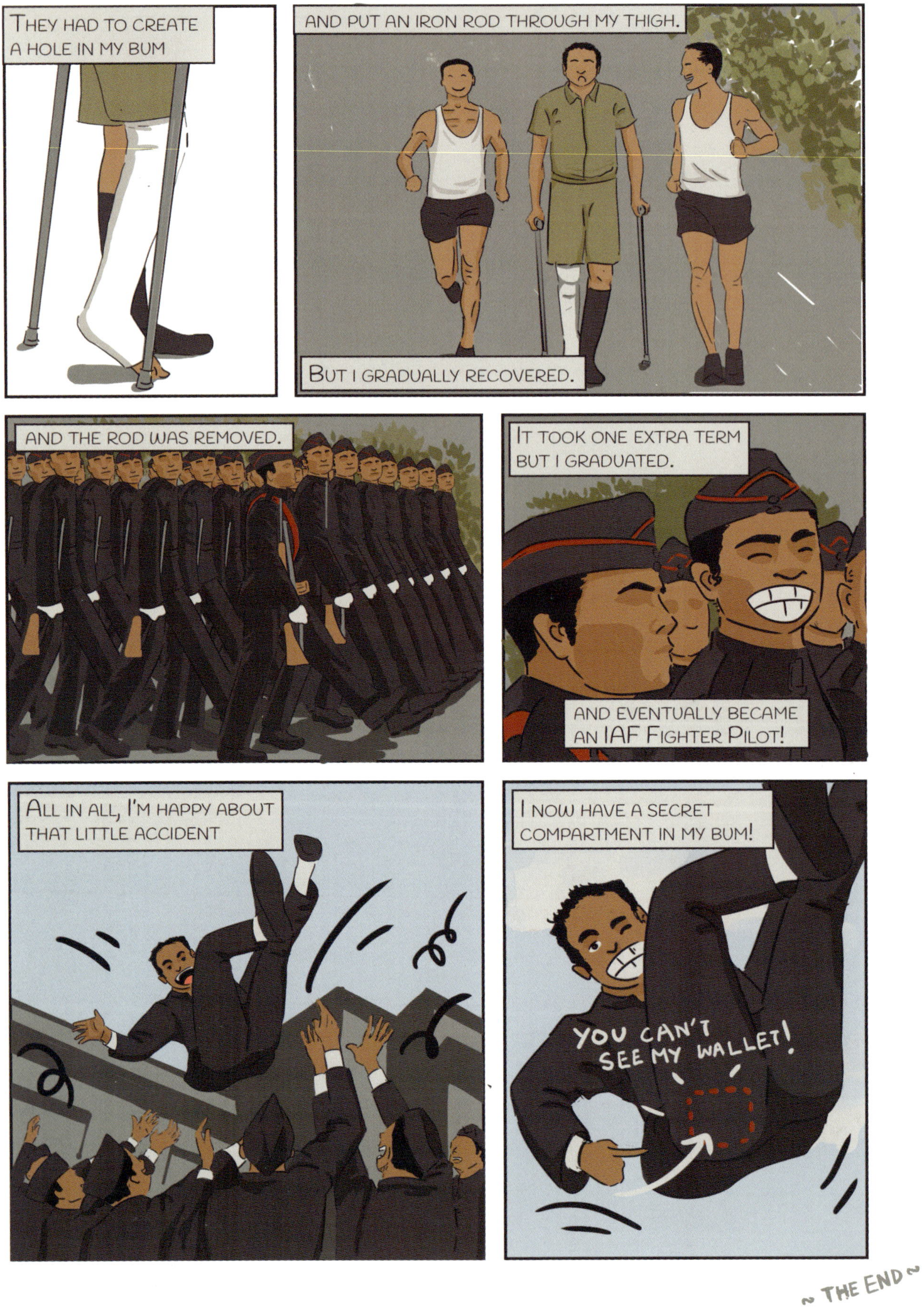

They had to create a hole in my bum
and put an iron rod through my thigh.
But I gradually recovered.
And the rod was removed.
It took one extra term but I graduated.
And eventually became an IAF Fighter Pilot!
All in all, I'm happy about that little accident
I now have a secret compartment in my bum!
YOU CAN'T SEE MY WALLET!
~ THE END ~

Meet the Ladies

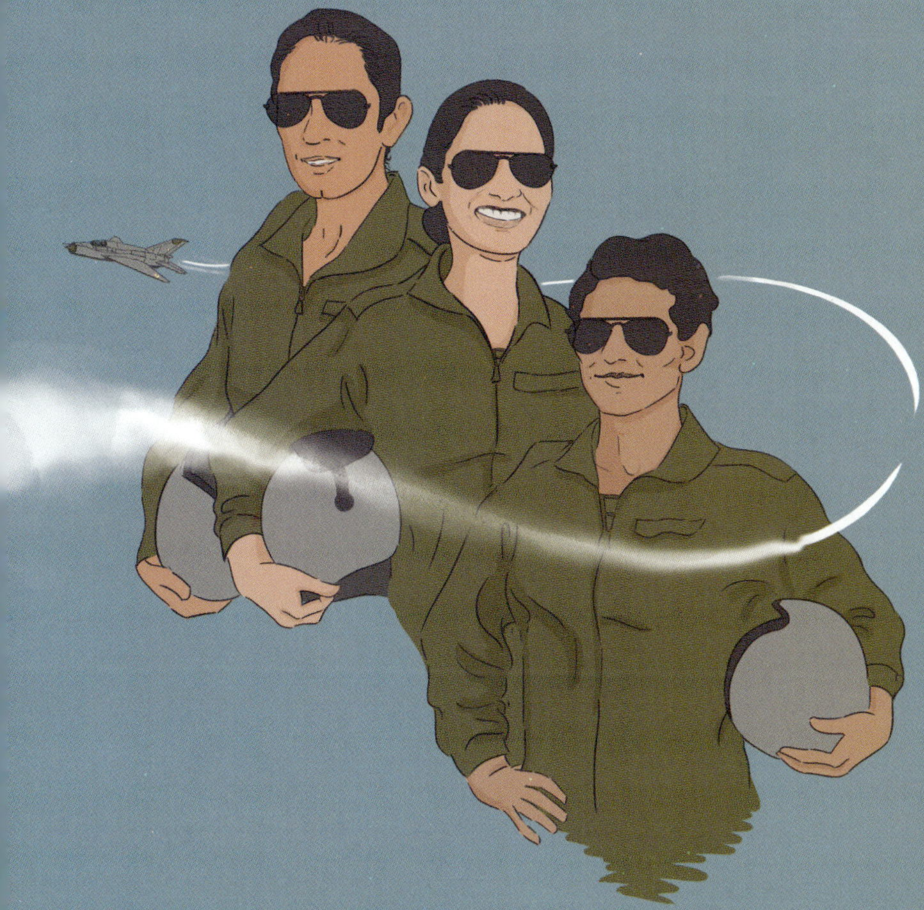

The IAF has had women as transport and helicopter pilots for over 20 years but in 2016, the IAF inducted its first batch of female fighter pilots — Mohana Singh, Avani Chaturvedi and Bhawana Kanth. The girls have become symbols of woman empowerment. Chaturvedi was the first amongst them to go solo on the MiG 21 Bison. All three girls completed engineering and then cleared AFCAT — the Air Force Common Admission Test to enter the IAF. As of now, women cannot join the IAF directly after school through NDA. Provisions for that to happen will need to be made but hopefully it's only a matter of time!

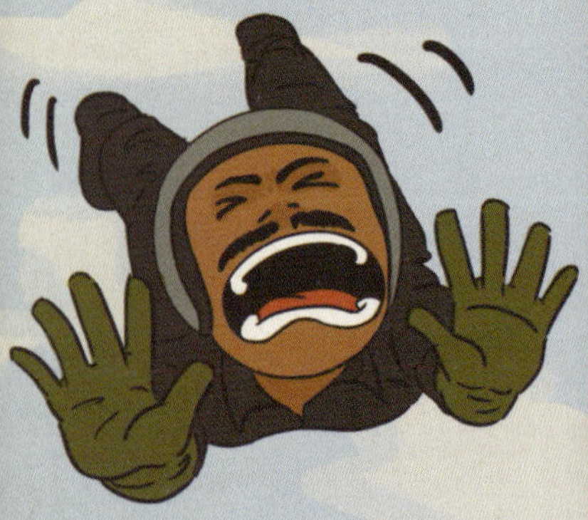

01

IT'S A BIRD, IT'S A PLANE, IT'S THE PILOT!

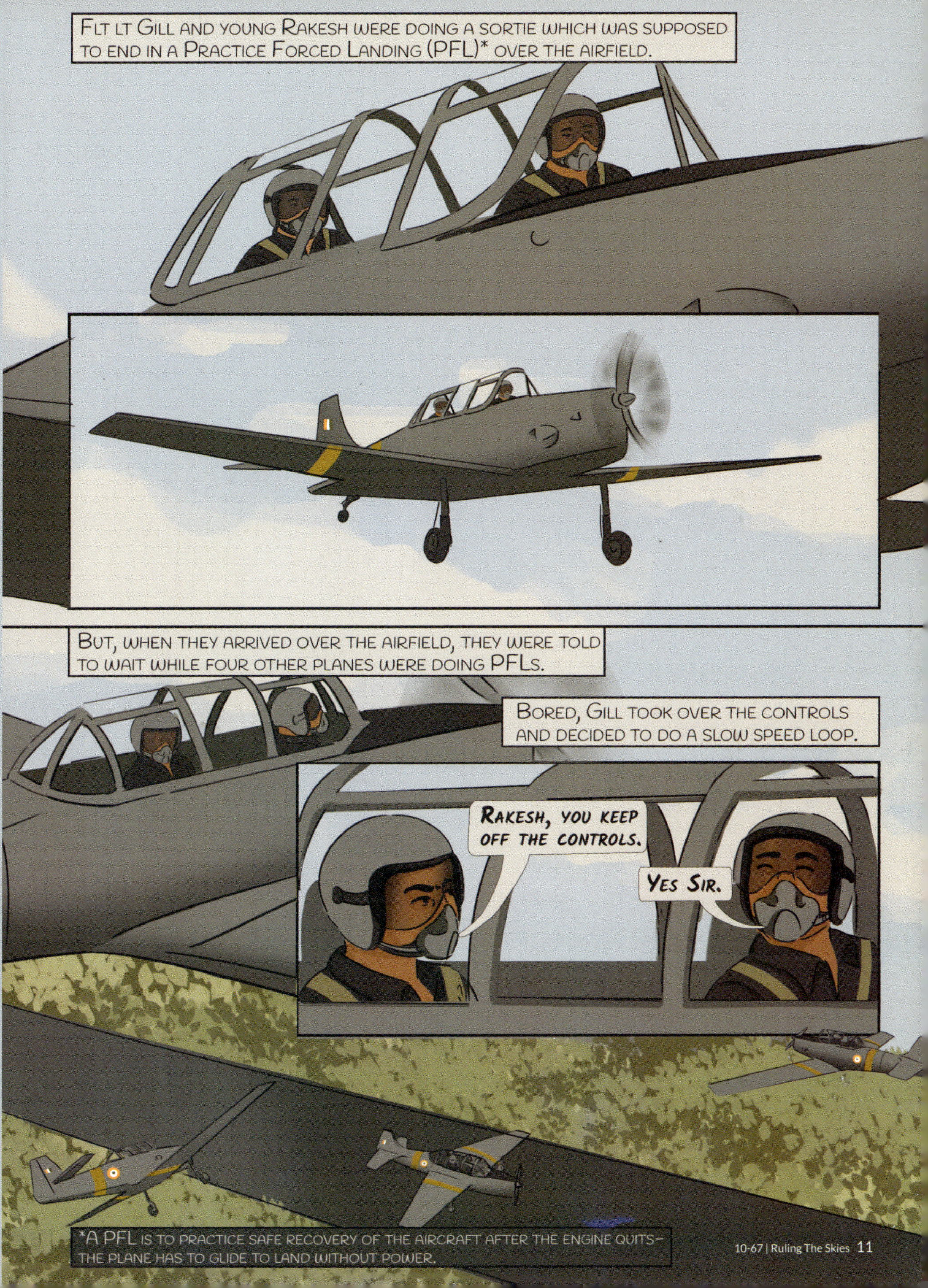
FLT LT GILL AND YOUNG RAKESH WERE DOING A SORTIE WHICH WAS SUPPOSED TO END IN A PRACTICE FORCED LANDING (PFL)* OVER THE AIRFIELD.
BUT, WHEN THEY ARRIVED OVER THE AIRFIELD, THEY WERE TOLD TO WAIT WHILE FOUR OTHER PLANES WERE DOING PFLS.
BORED, GILL TOOK OVER THE CONTROLS AND DECIDED TO DO A SLOW SPEED LOOP.
RAKESH, YOU KEEP OFF THE CONTROLS.
YES SIR.
*A PFL IS TO PRACTICE SAFE RECOVERY OF THE AIRCRAFT AFTER THE ENGINE QUITS– THE PLANE HAS TO GLIDE TO LAND WITHOUT POWER.

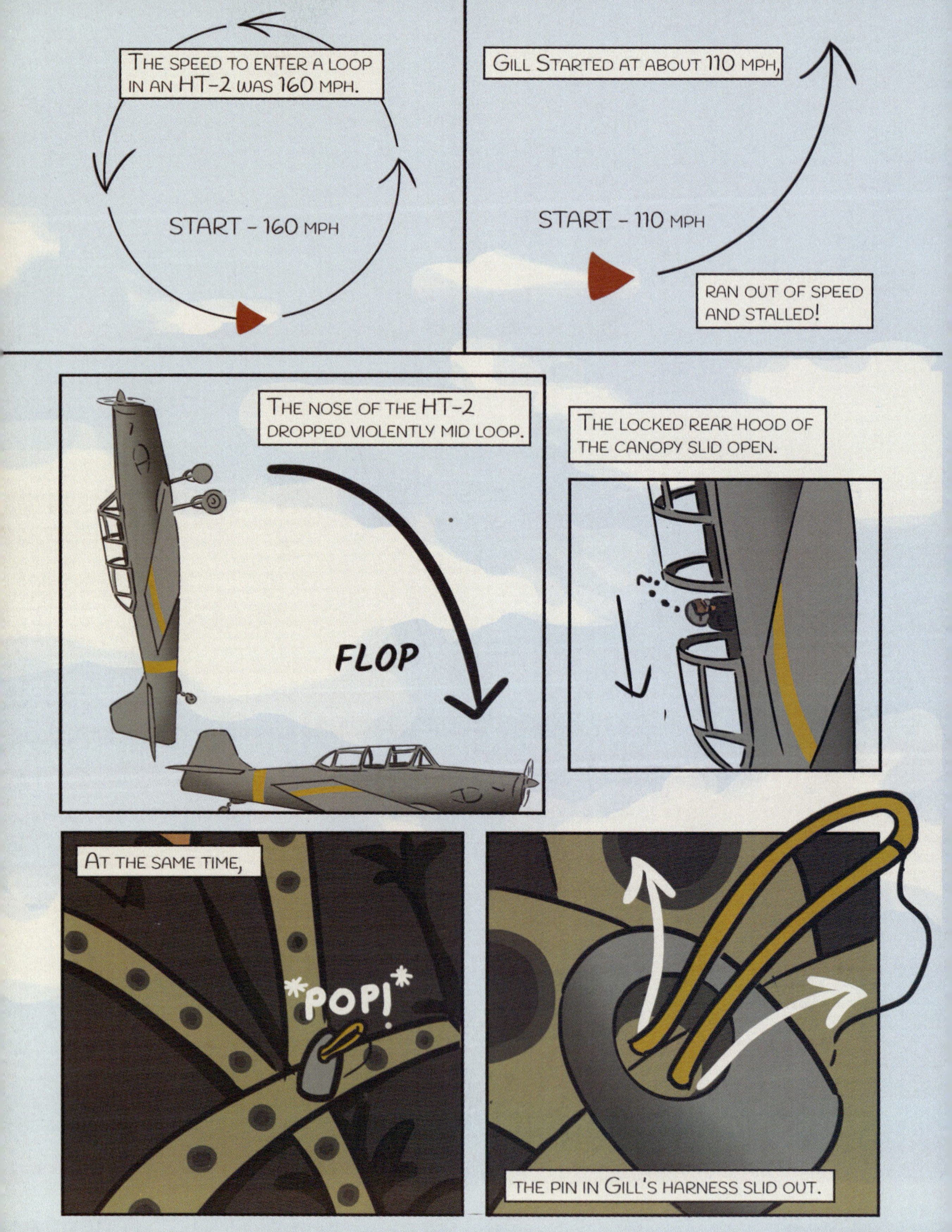
THE SPEED TO ENTER A LOOP IN AN HT-2 WAS 160 MPH.
START - 160 MPH
GILL STARTED AT ABOUT 110 MPH,
START - 110 MPH
RAN OUT OF SPEED AND STALLED!
THE NOSE OF THE HT-2 DROPPED VIOLENTLY MID LOOP.
FLOP
THE LOCKED REAR HOOD OF THE CANOPY SLID OPEN.
AT THE SAME TIME,
POP!
THE PIN IN GILL'S HARNESS SLID OUT.

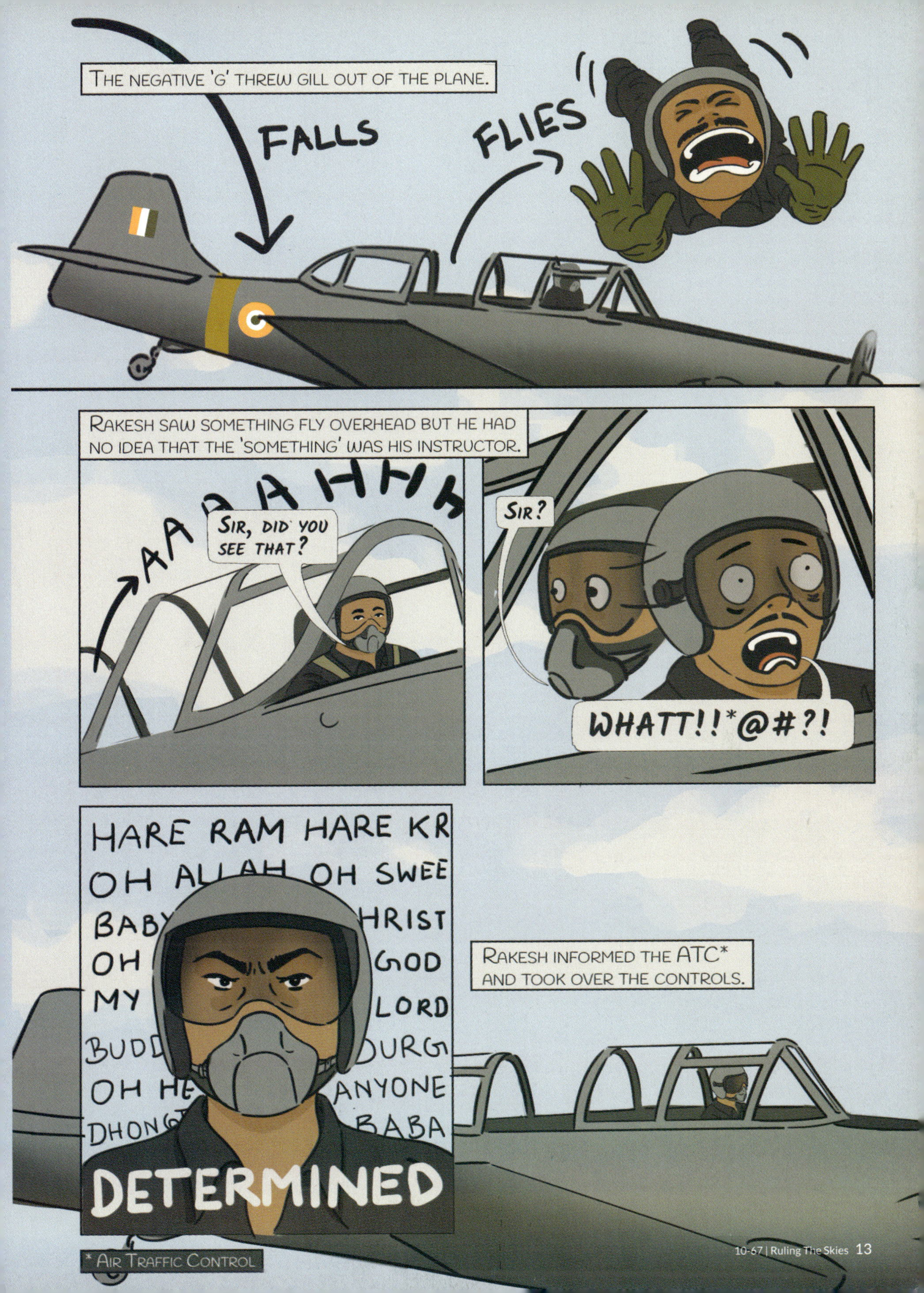

THE NEGATIVE 'G' THREW GILL OUT OF THE PLANE.
FALLS
FLIES
RAKESH SAW SOMETHING FLY OVERHEAD BUT HE HAD NO IDEA THAT THE 'SOMETHING' WAS HIS INSTRUCTOR.
AAAAHHH
SIR, DID YOU SEE THAT?
SIR?
WHATT!!*@#?!
HARE RAM HARE KR
OH ALLAH OH SWEE
BABY
HRIST
OH
GOD
MY
LORD
BUDD
DURG
OH HE
ANYONE
DHON
BABA
DETERMINED
RAKESH INFORMED THE ATC* AND TOOK OVER THE CONTROLS.
* AIR TRAFFIC CONTROL

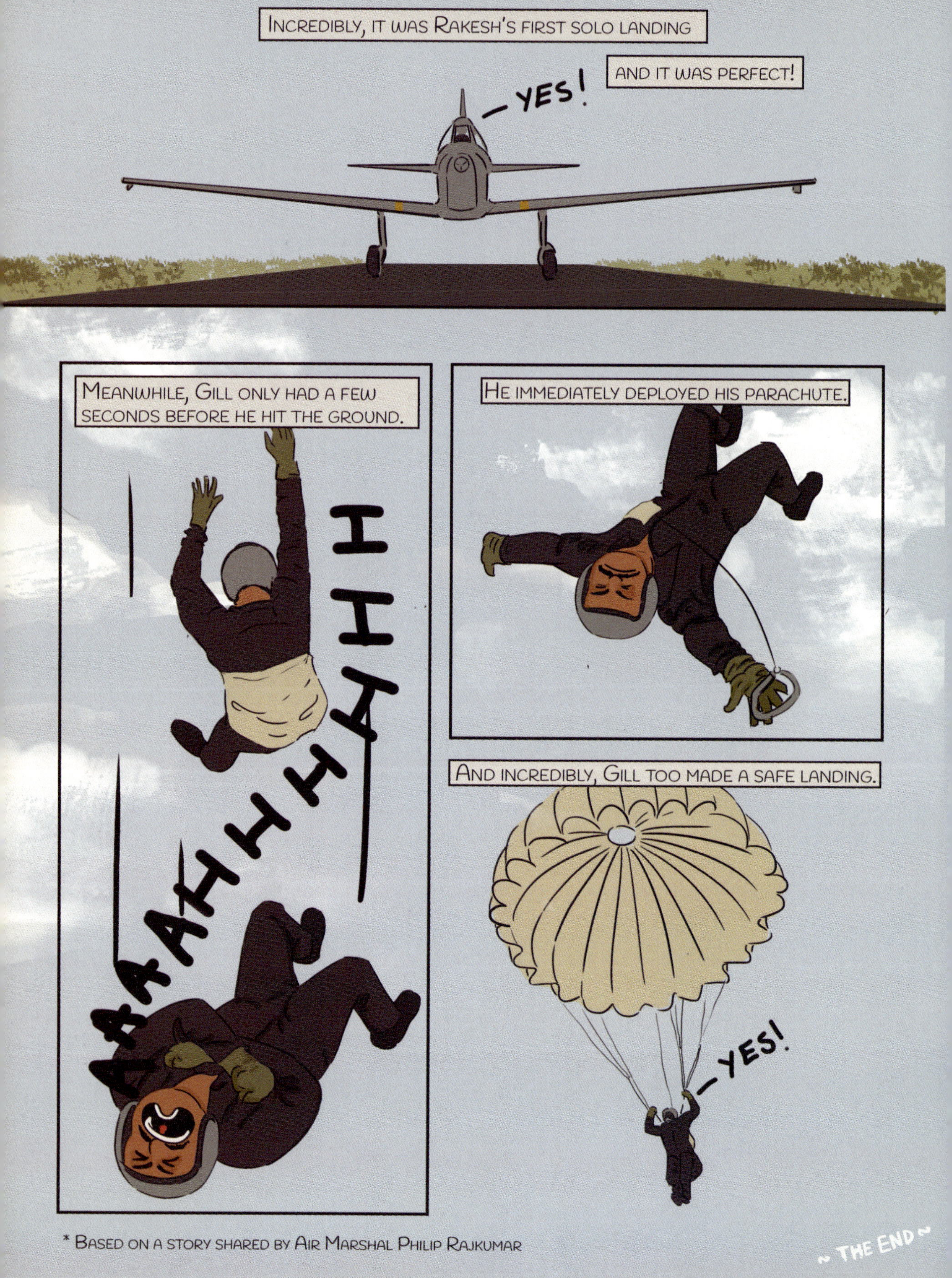

* Based on a story shared by Air Marshal Philip Rajkumar

Fighter Trivia: The HAL HT-2

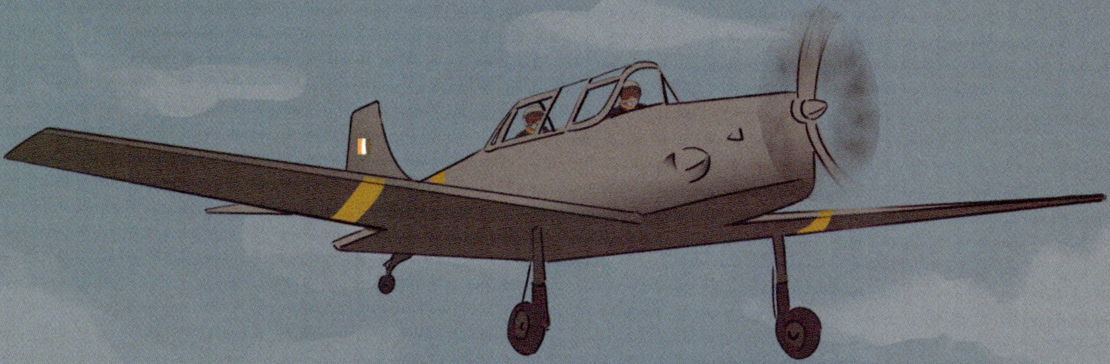

The HT-2 was a two-seater trainer. Unlike the MiGs or other fighter jets, trainers like the HT-2 and Kiran do not reach supersonic speeds. In these planes the pilots do not wear anti-g suits. Anti g-suits are worn by aviators and astronauts to protect them against high levels of acceleration force (g) which can cause blackouts and accidents. In the trainers, pilots only wear their regular flying overalls.

In the HT-2, pilots did not "eject", they "bailed out". The parachutes were not built into the seats but worn by the pilots. In case of an emergency, the canopy could be opened and the pilot would have to climb out onto the wing and jump from there. Naturally, the pilots and the aircraft canopy are secured more safely in fighter jets unlike trainers. Nothing about the scenario told in the last story could ever happen on a MiG or on any other modern fighter jet.

In conversation with Fighter Pilots #1

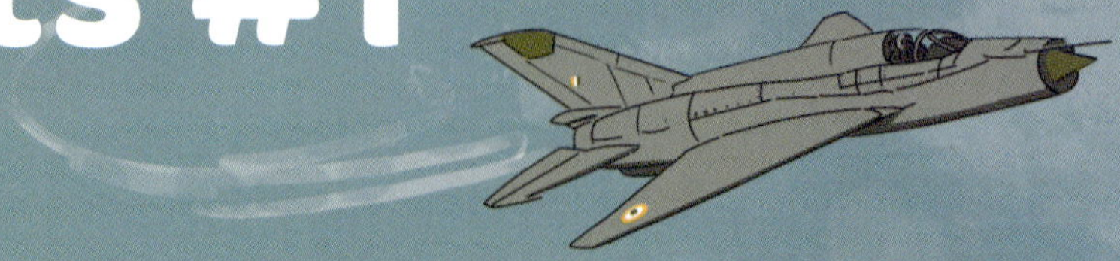

“What made you want to fly fighter planes? What is so special about it?”

Rusty “It’s unique. The sky is the limit. No one else does or can do or is permitted to do what fighter pilots do.”

DS “It’s the most fun thing to do in the world...There’s this word, “Kinesthetics” - Kinetics and aesthetics - It is the beauty of motion.”

Mukho “I can’t explain...you’ve got to do it to know it.
It’s addictive.”

Sunil “I think it is a very great personal sense of achievement when you achieve milestones like the first solo flight, first night solo, first weapon you fire, a good range score or a good combat sortie.
Its akin to what a mountaineer feels when he scales the Everest.”

02

A QUICK CRASH COURSE

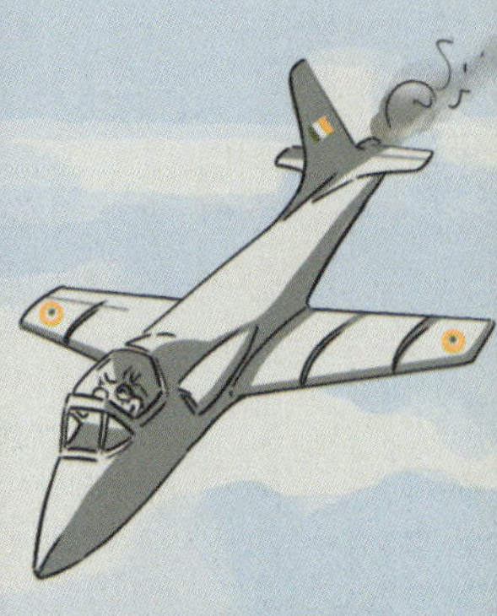

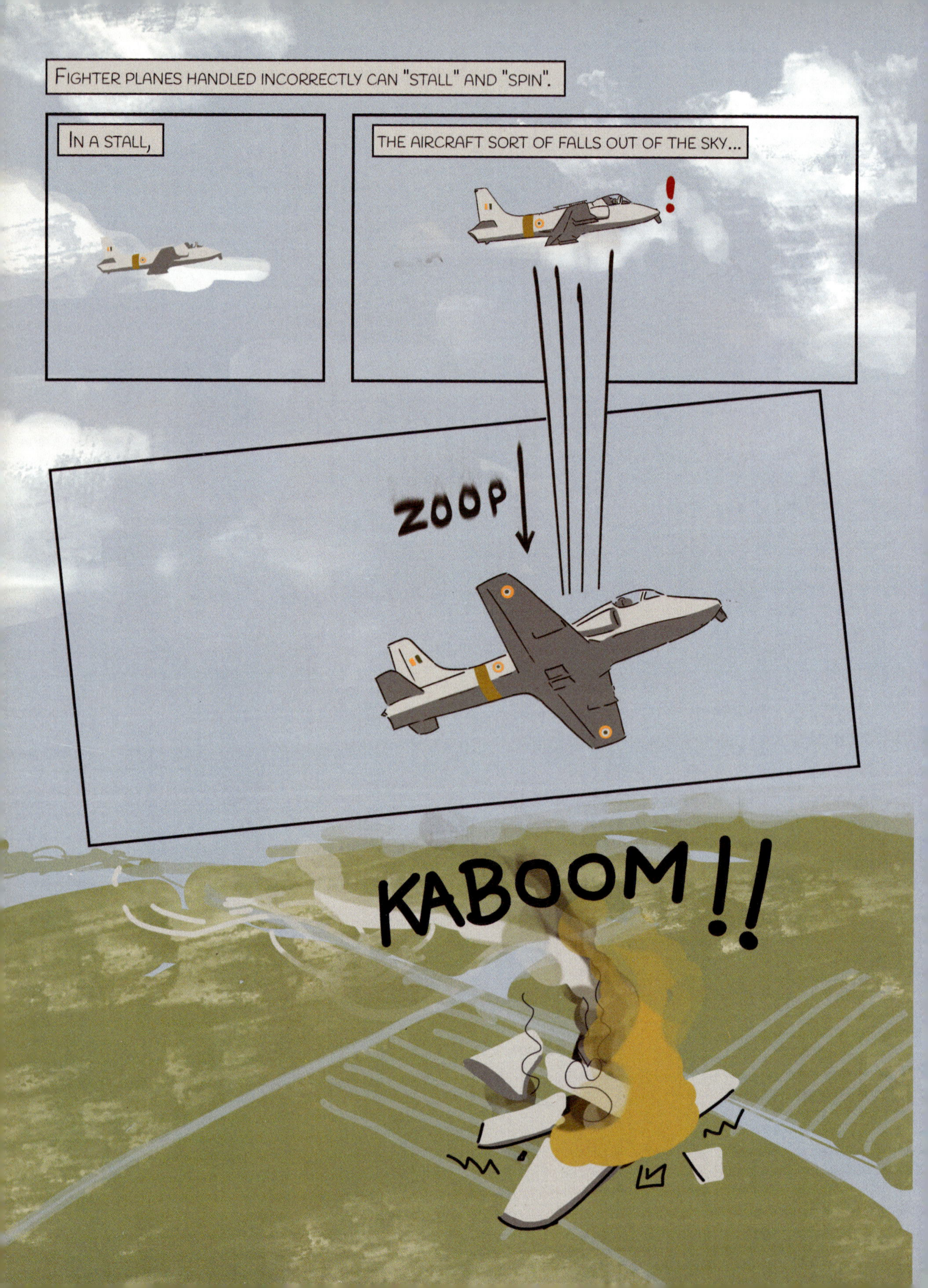
FIGHTER PLANES HANDLED INCORRECTLY CAN "STALL" AND "SPIN".
IN A STALL,
THE AIRCRAFT SORT OF FALLS OUT OF THE SKY...
!
ZOOP
KABOOM!!

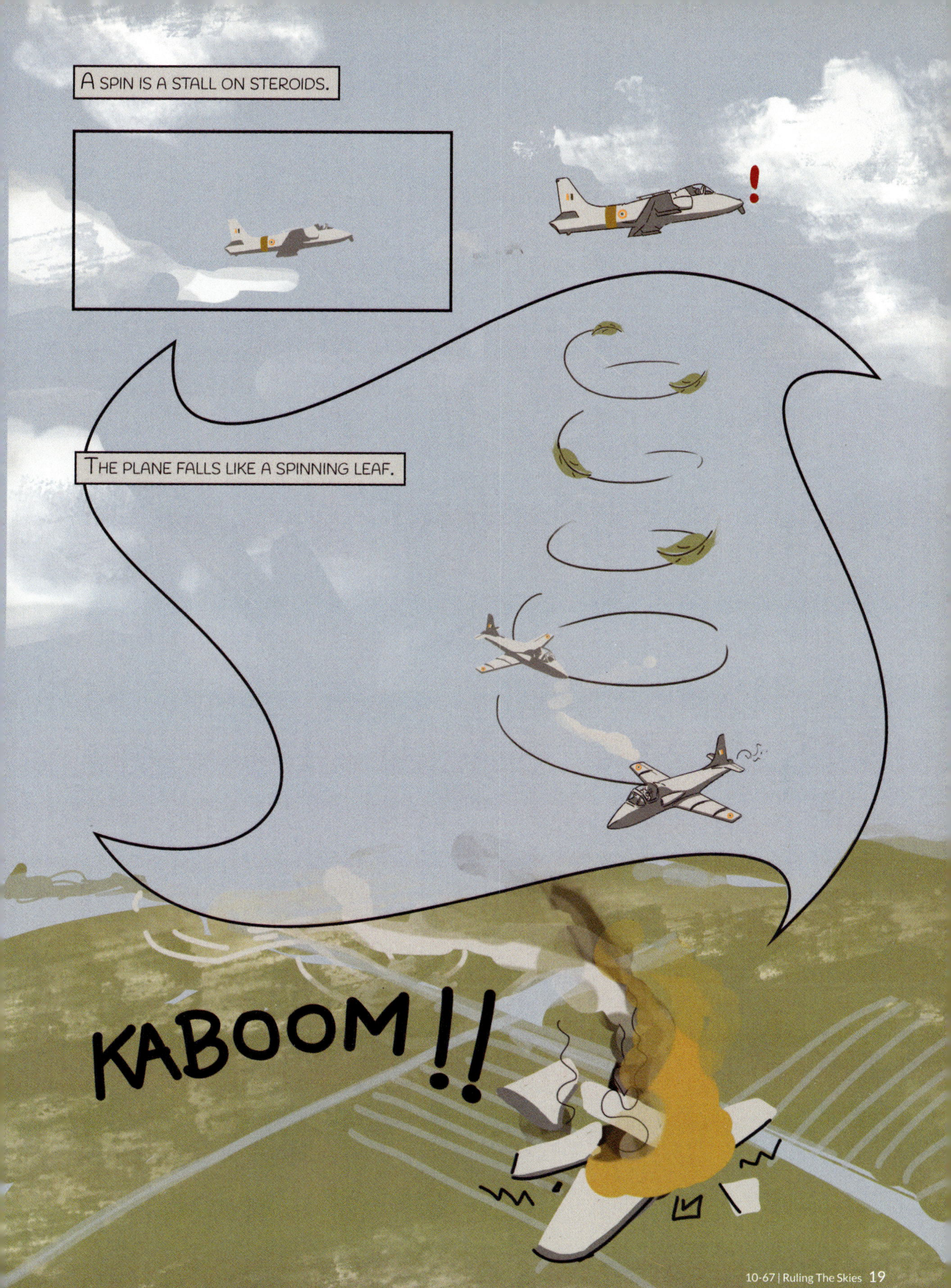
A SPIN IS A STALL ON STEROIDS.
!
THE PLANE FALLS LIKE A SPINNING LEAF.
KABOOM!!

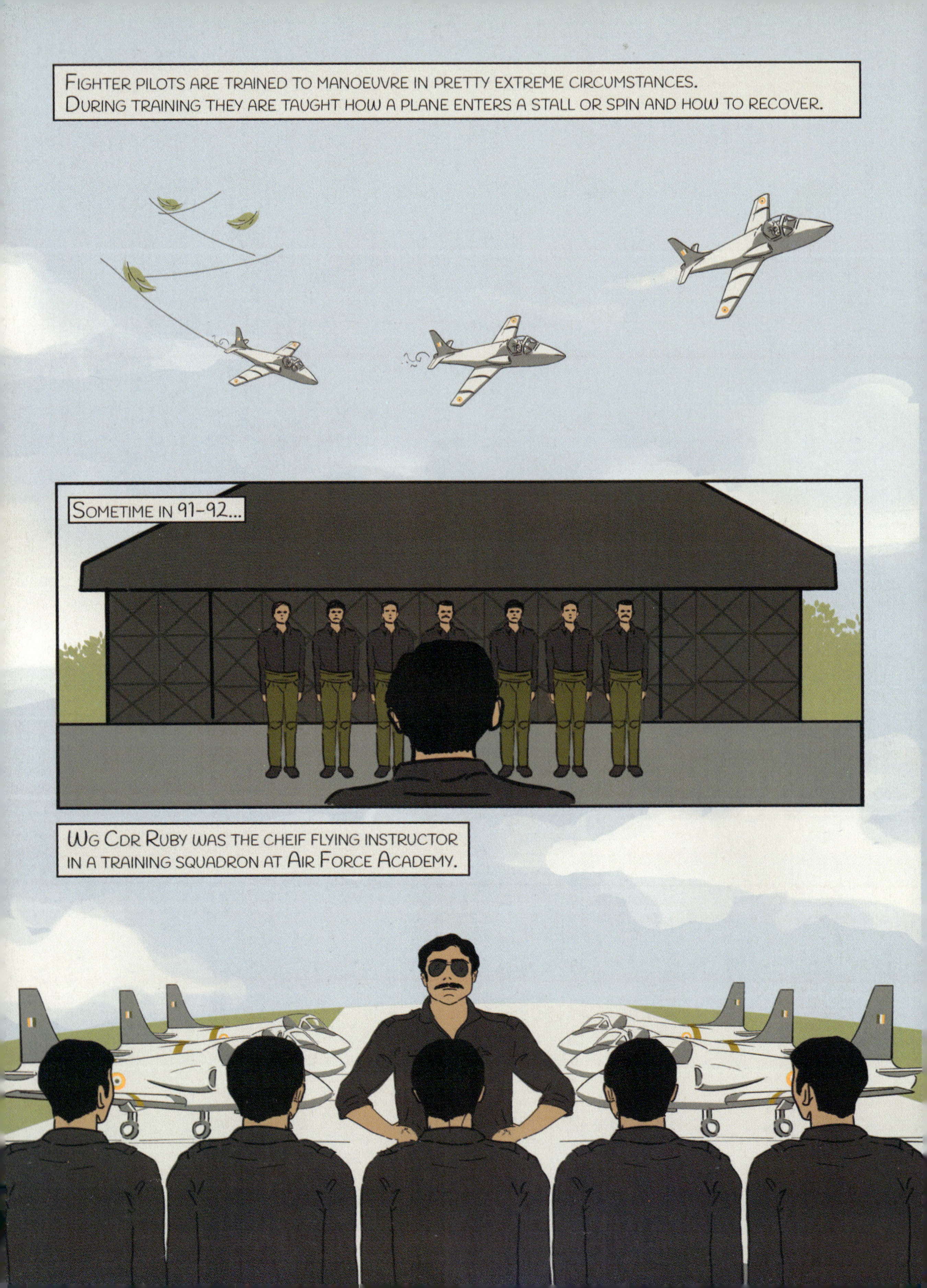
FIGHTER PILOTS ARE TRAINED TO MANOEUVRE IN PRETTY EXTREME CIRCUMSTANCES.
DURING TRAINING THEY ARE TAUGHT HOW A PLANE ENTERS A STALL OR SPIN AND HOW TO RECOVER.
SOMETIME IN 91–92...
WG CDR RUBY WAS THE CHEIF FLYING INSTRUCTOR IN A TRAINING SQUADRON AT AIR FORCE ACADEMY.

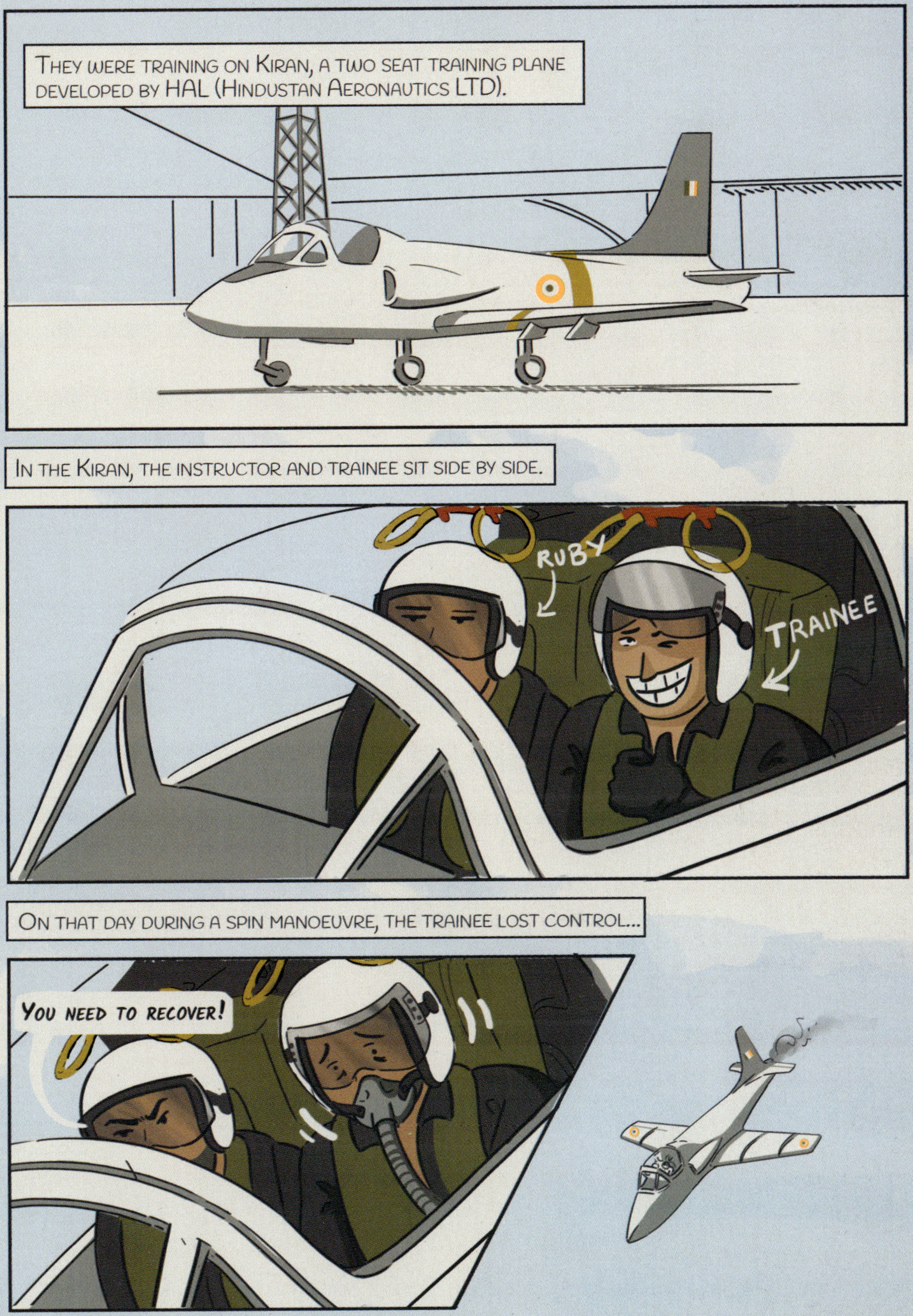
THEY WERE TRAINING ON KIRAN, A TWO SEAT TRAINING PLANE DEVELOPED BY HAL (HINDUSTAN AERONAUTICS LTD).
IN THE KIRAN, THE INSTRUCTOR AND TRAINEE SIT SIDE BY SIDE.
RUBY
TRAINEE
ON THAT DAY DURING A SPIN MANOEUVRE, THE TRAINEE LOST CONTROL...
YOU NEED TO RECOVER!

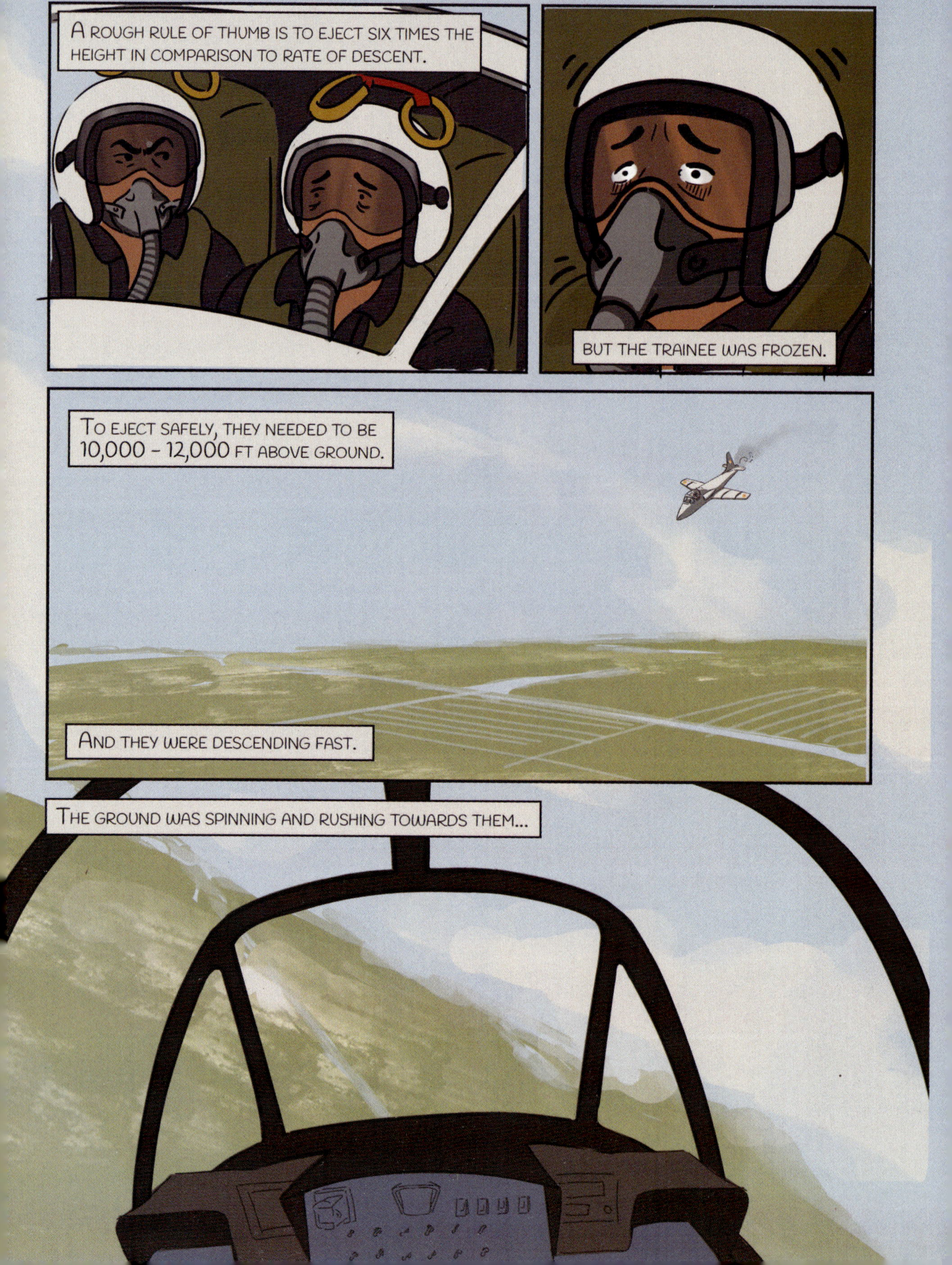
A ROUGH RULE OF THUMB IS TO EJECT SIX TIMES THE HEIGHT IN COMPARISON TO RATE OF DESCENT.
BUT THE TRAINEE WAS FROZEN.
TO EJECT SAFELY, THEY NEEDED TO BE 10,000 - 12,000 FT ABOVE GROUND.
AND THEY WERE DESCENDING FAST.
THE GROUND WAS SPINNING AND RUSHING TOWARDS THEM...

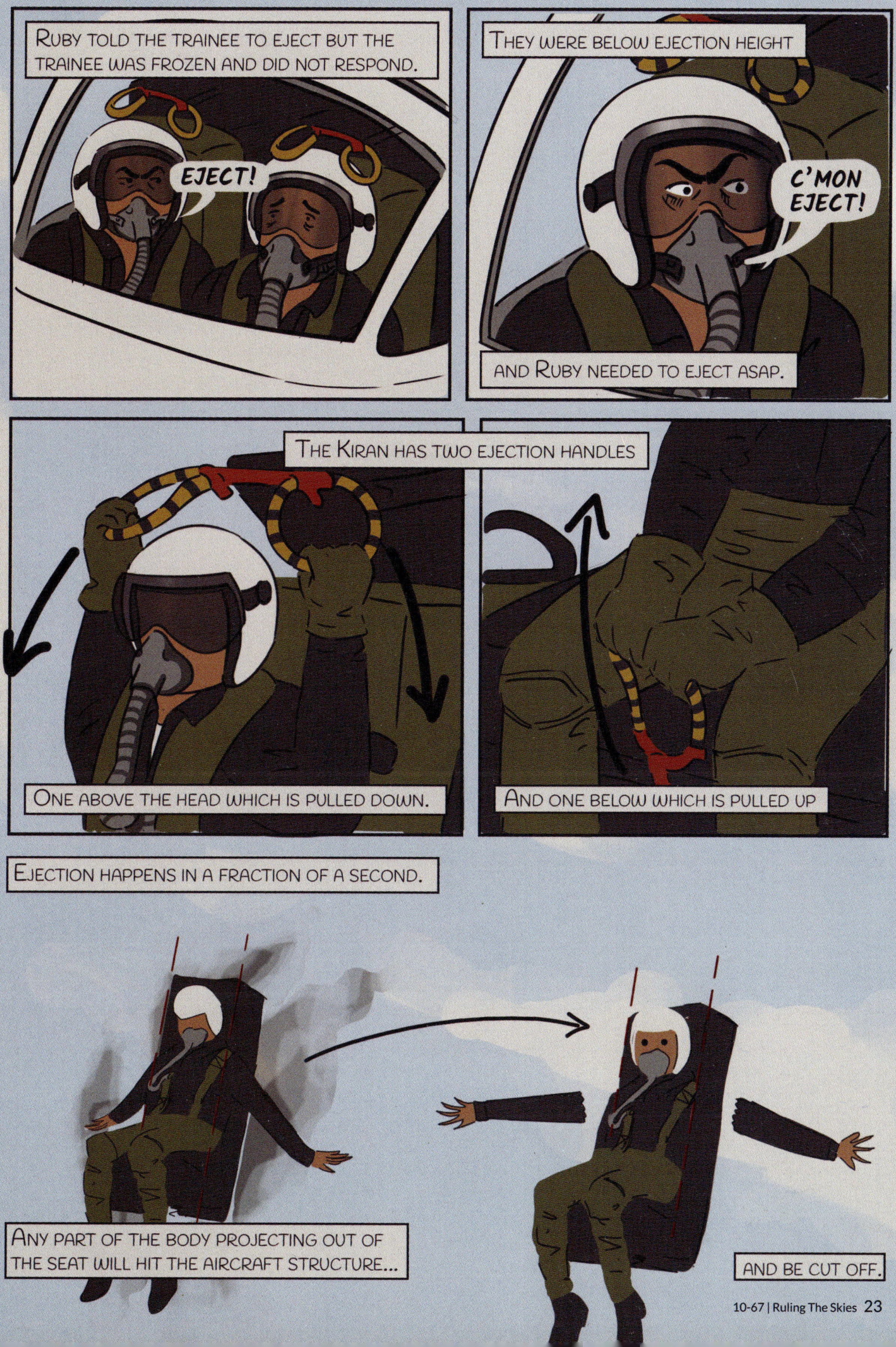
RUBY TOLD THE TRAINEE TO EJECT BUT THE TRAINEE WAS FROZEN AND DID NOT RESPOND.
EJECT!
THEY WERE BELOW EJECTION HEIGHT
C'MON EJECT!
AND RUBY NEEDED TO EJECT ASAP.
THE KIRAN HAS TWO EJECTION HANDLES
ONE ABOVE THE HEAD WHICH IS PULLED DOWN.
AND ONE BELOW WHICH IS PULLED UP
EJECTION HAPPENS IN A FRACTION OF A SECOND.
ANY PART OF THE BODY PROJECTING OUT OF THE SEAT WILL HIT THE AIRCRAFT STRUCTURE...
AND BE CUT OFF.

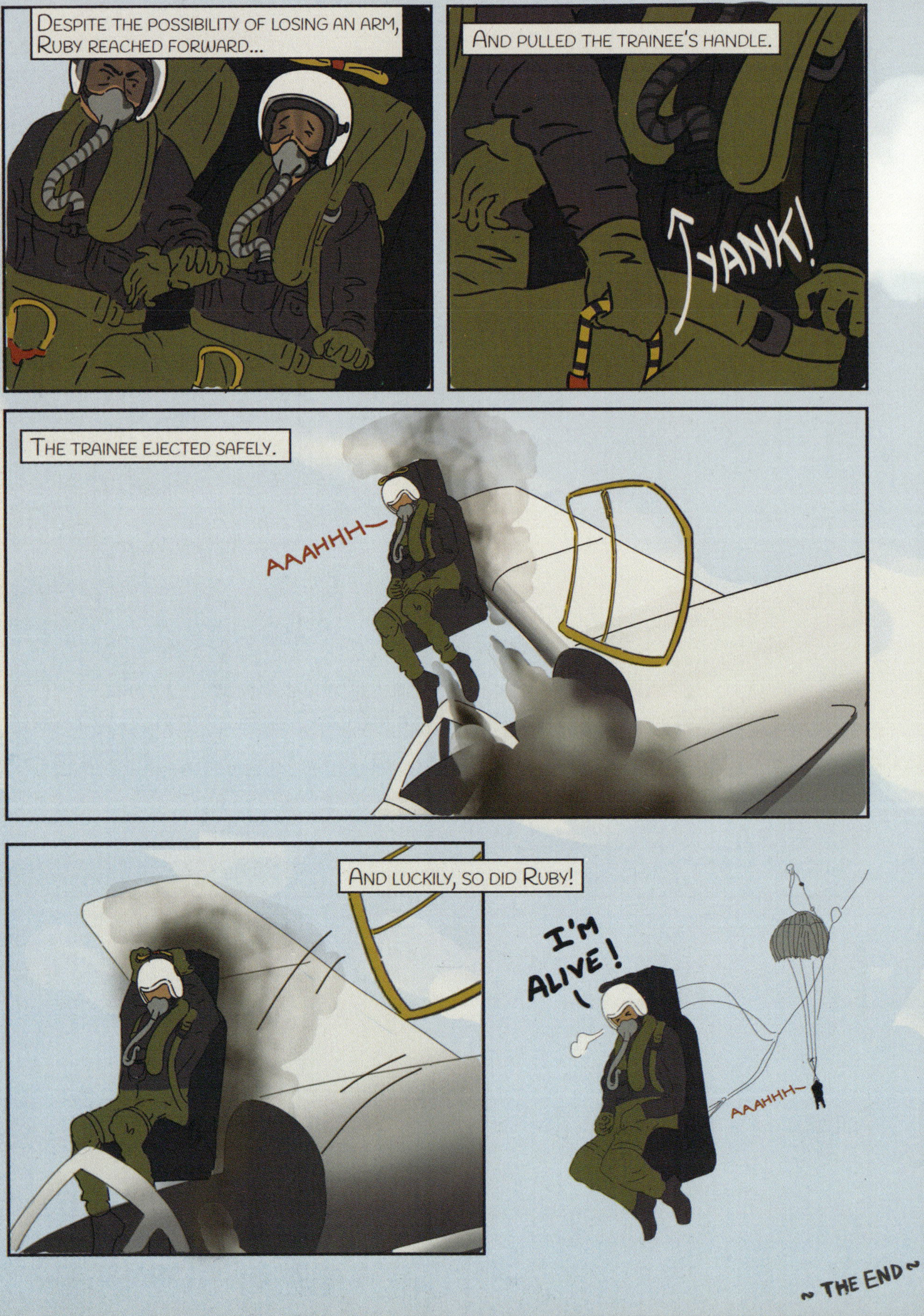
DESPITE THE POSSIBILITY OF LOSING AN ARM, RUBY REACHED FORWARD...
AND PULLED THE TRAINEE'S HANDLE.
YANK!
THE TRAINEE EJECTED SAFELY.
AAAHHH~
AND LUCKILY, SO DID RUBY!
I'M ALIVE!
AAAHHH~
~ THE END ~

03

A CLOSE CALL

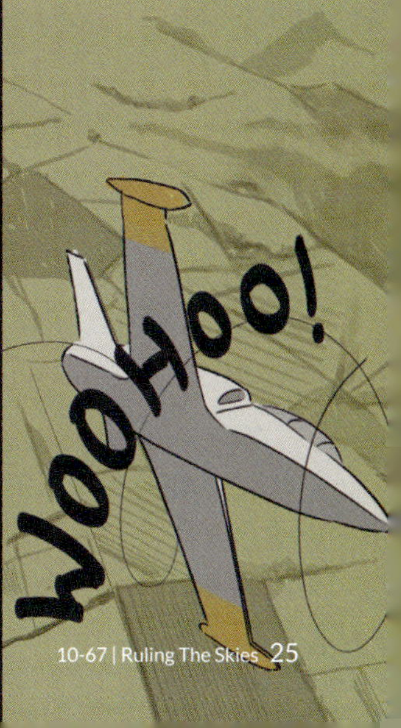

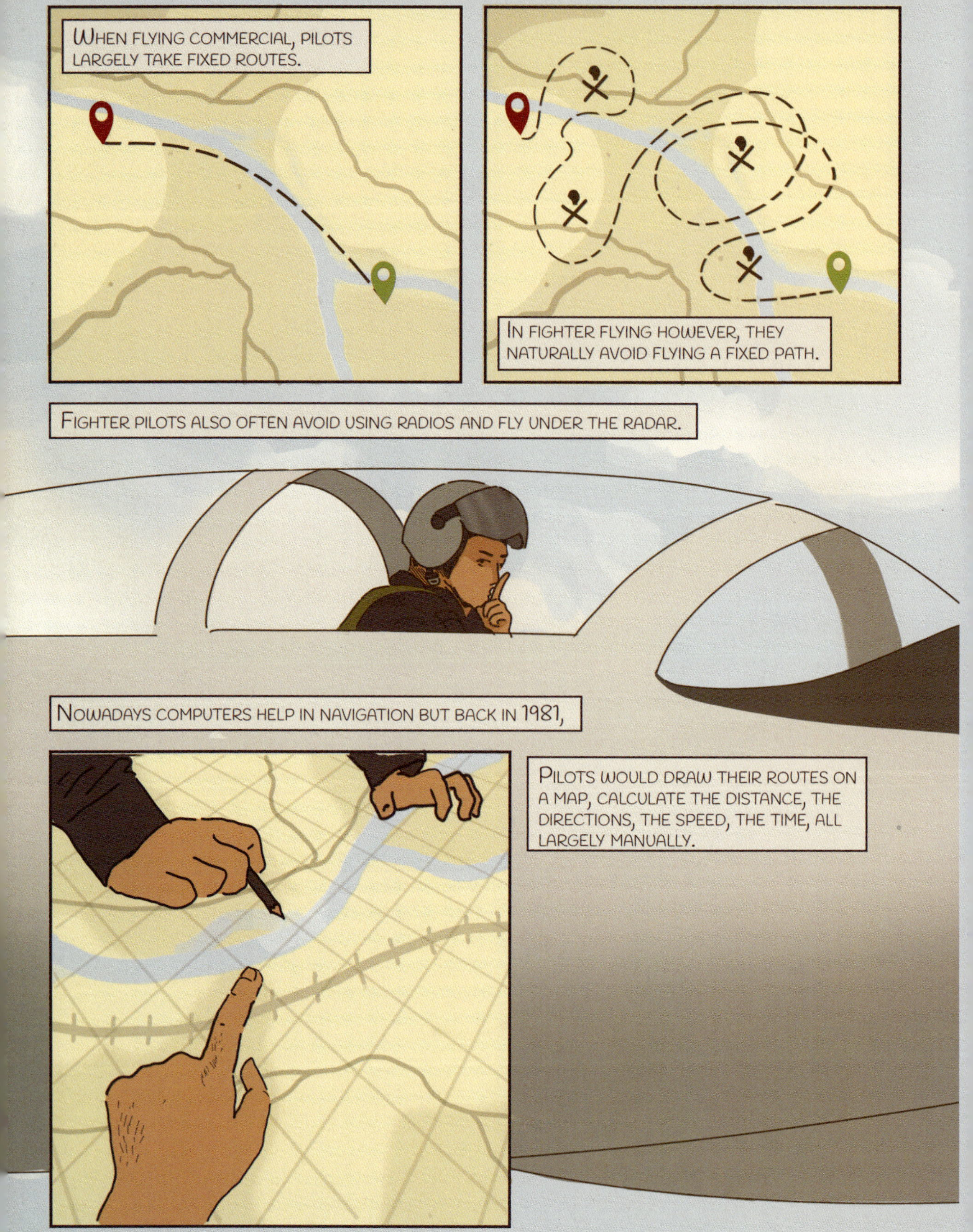
WHEN FLYING COMMERCIAL, PILOTS LARGELY TAKE FIXED ROUTES.
IN FIGHTER FLYING HOWEVER, THEY NATURALLY AVOID FLYING A FIXED PATH.
FIGHTER PILOTS ALSO OFTEN AVOID USING RADIOS AND FLY UNDER THE RADAR.
NOWADAYS COMPUTERS HELP IN NAVIGATION BUT BACK IN 1981,
PILOTS WOULD DRAW THEIR ROUTES ON A MAP, CALCULATE THE DISTANCE, THE DIRECTIONS, THE SPEED, THE TIME, ALL LARGELY MANUALLY.

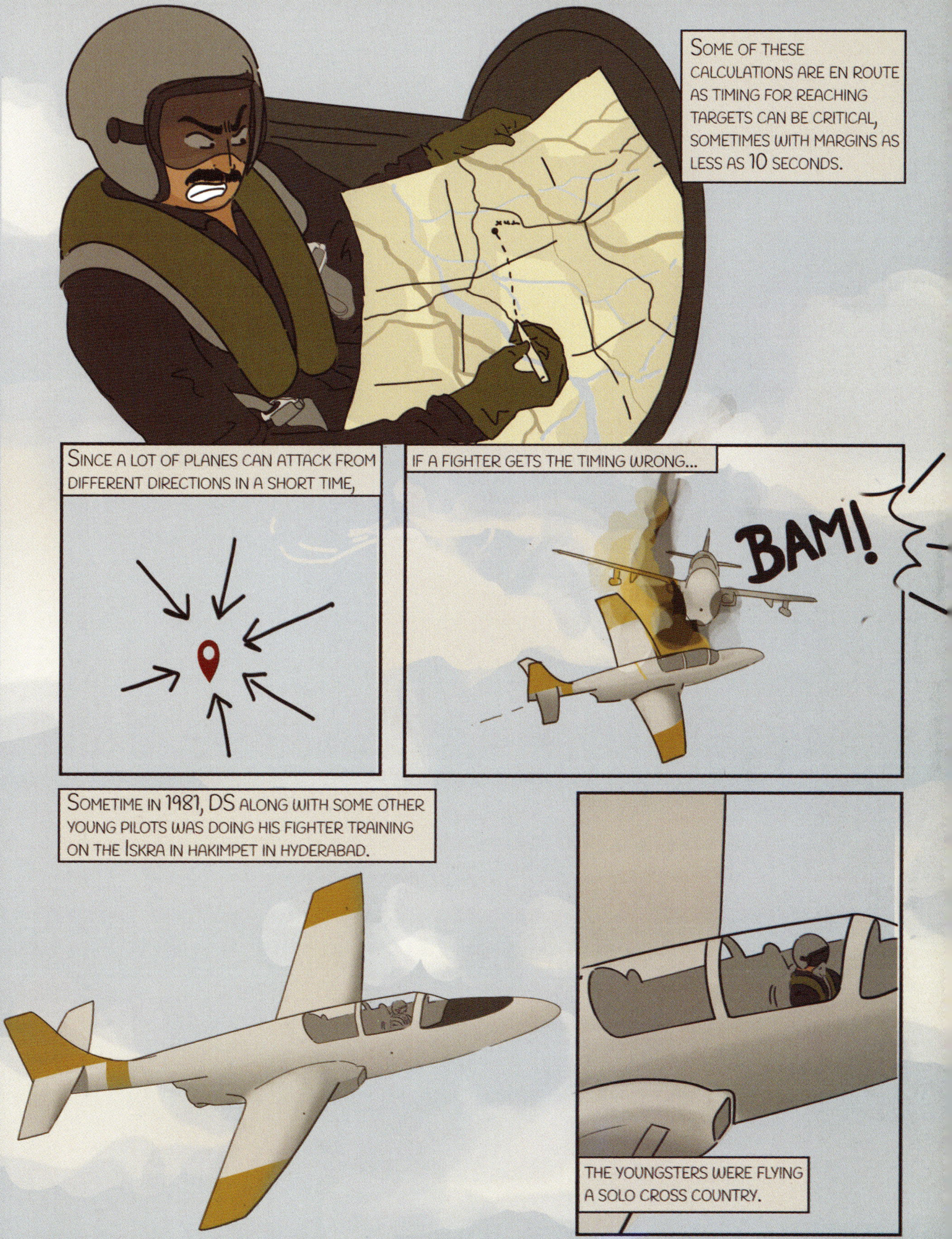
SOME OF THESE CALCULATIONS ARE EN ROUTE AS TIMING FOR REACHING TARGETS CAN BE CRITICAL, SOMETIMES WITH MARGINS AS LESS AS 10 SECONDS.
SINCE A LOT OF PLANES CAN ATTACK FROM DIFFERENT DIRECTIONS IN A SHORT TIME,
IF A FIGHTER GETS THE TIMING WRONG...
BAM!
SOMETIME IN 1981, DS ALONG WITH SOME OTHER YOUNG PILOTS WAS DOING HIS FIGHTER TRAINING ON THE ISKRA IN HAKIMPET IN HYDERABAD.
THE YOUNGSTERS WERE FLYING A SOLO CROSS COUNTRY.

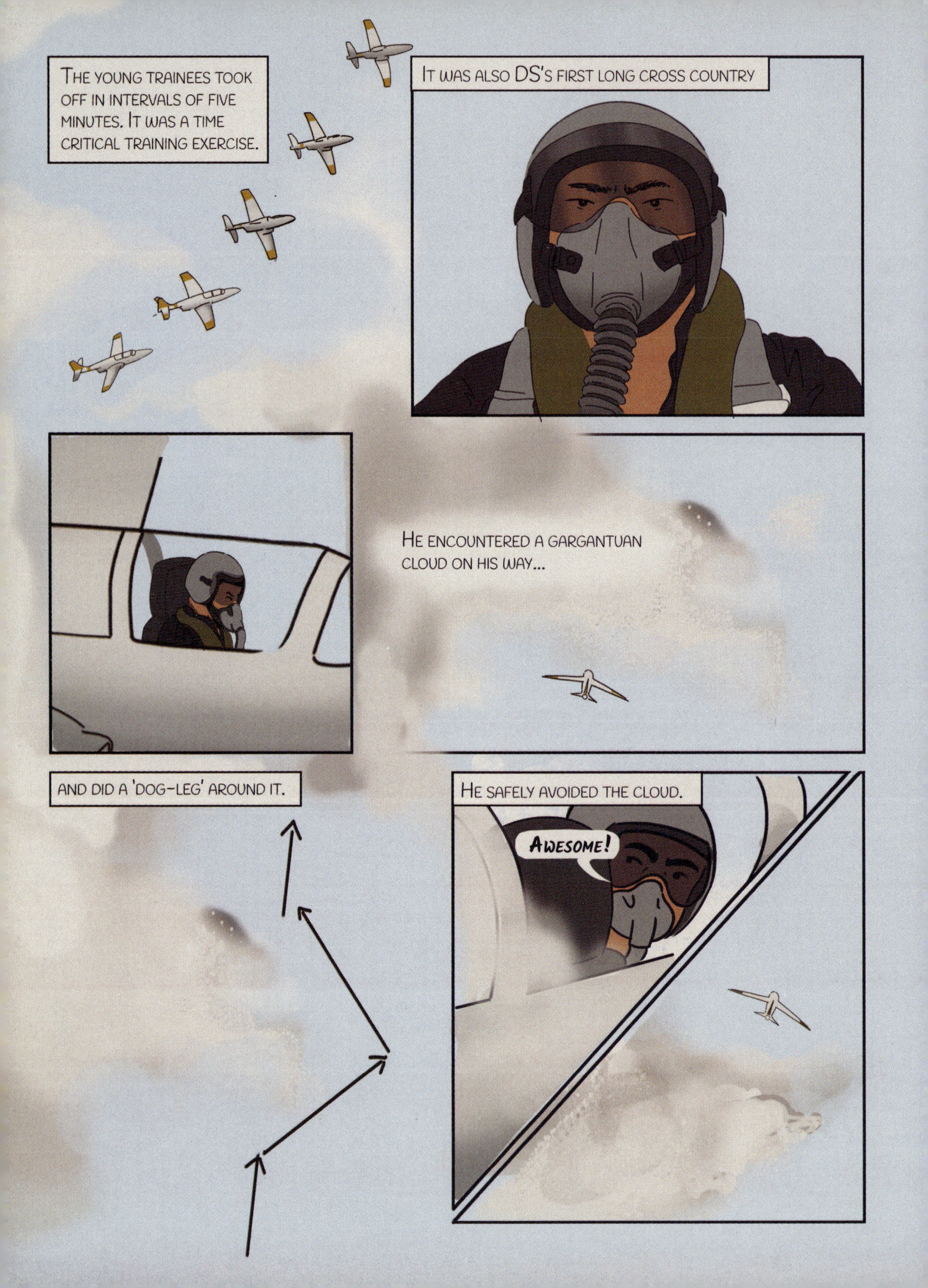
THE YOUNG TRAINEES TOOK OFF IN INTERVALS OF FIVE MINUTES. IT WAS A TIME CRITICAL TRAINING EXERCISE.
IT WAS ALSO DS'S FIRST LONG CROSS COUNTRY
HE ENCOUNTERED A GARGANTUAN CLOUD ON HIS WAY...
AND DID A 'DOG-LEG' AROUND IT.
HE SAFELY AVOIDED THE CLOUD.
AWESOME!

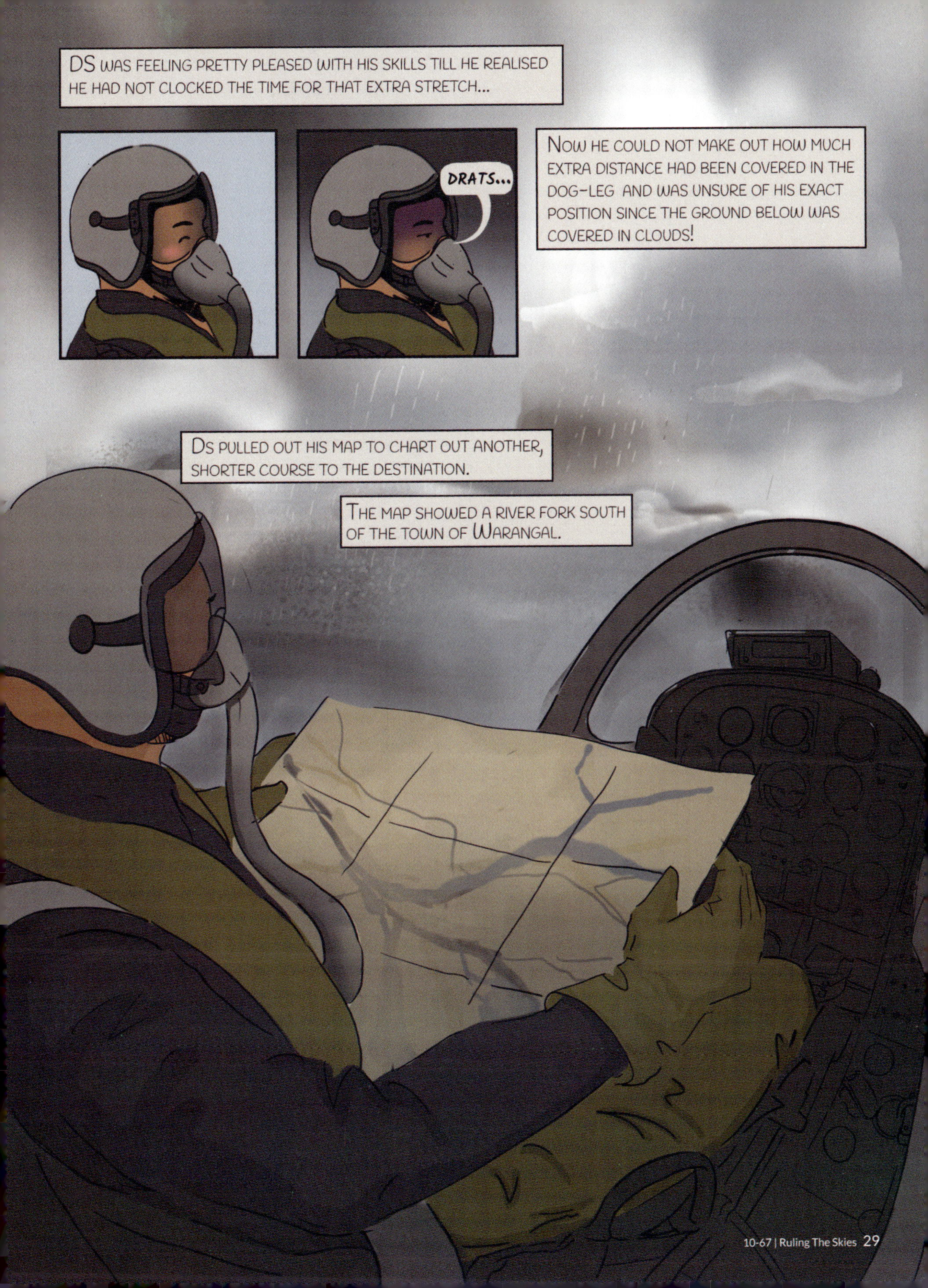
DS WAS FEELING PRETTY PLEASED WITH HIS SKILLS TILL HE REALISED HE HAD NOT CLOCKED THE TIME FOR THAT EXTRA STRETCH...
DRATS...
NOW HE COULD NOT MAKE OUT HOW MUCH EXTRA DISTANCE HAD BEEN COVERED IN THE DOG-LEG AND WAS UNSURE OF HIS EXACT POSITION SINCE THE GROUND BELOW WAS COVERED IN CLOUDS!
DS PULLED OUT HIS MAP TO CHART OUT ANOTHER, SHORTER COURSE TO THE DESTINATION.
THE MAP SHOWED A RIVER FORK SOUTH OF THE TOWN OF WARANGAL.

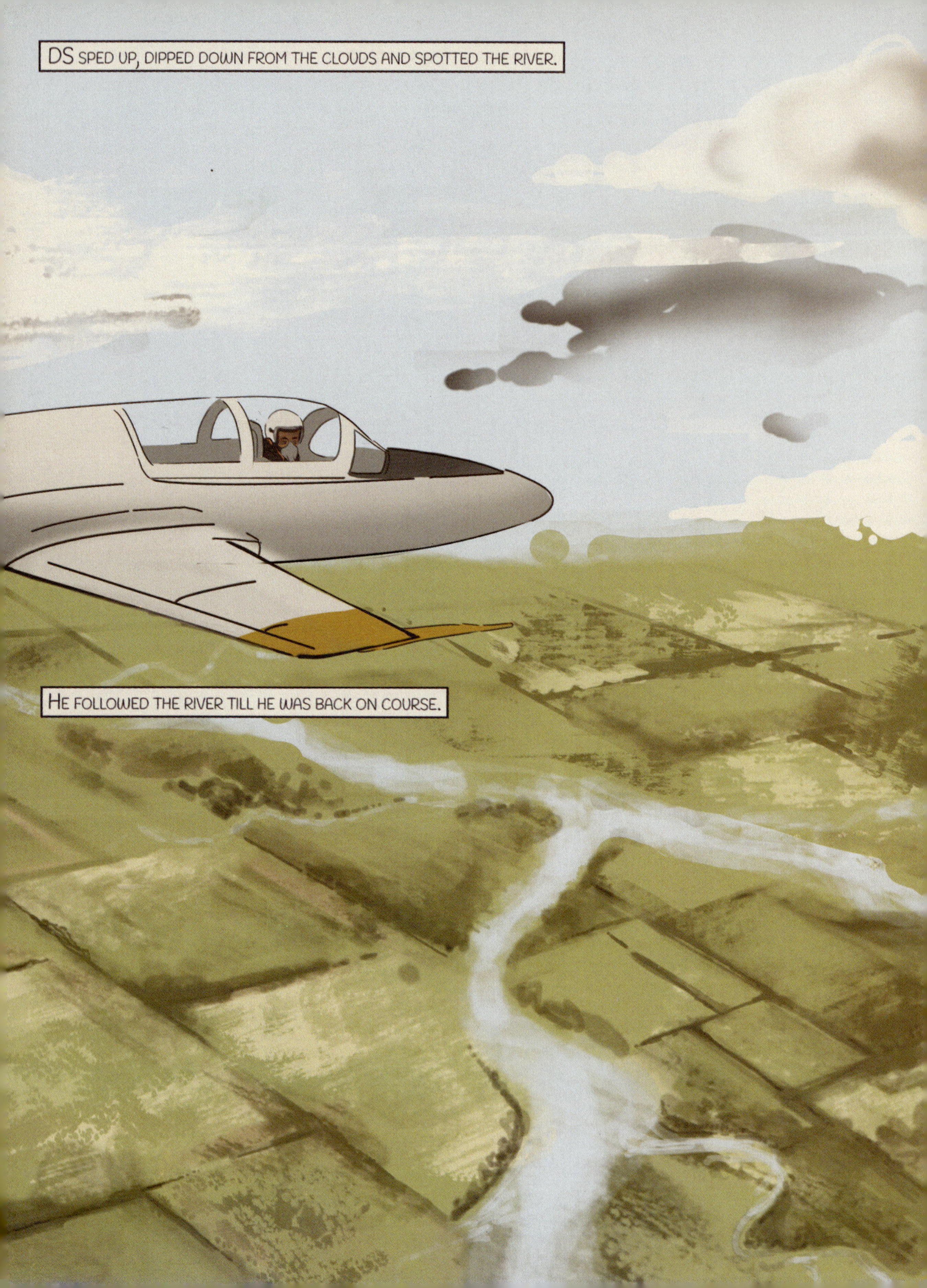
DS SPED UP, DIPPED DOWN FROM THE CLOUDS AND SPOTTED THE RIVER.
HE FOLLOWED THE RIVER TILL HE WAS BACK ON COURSE.

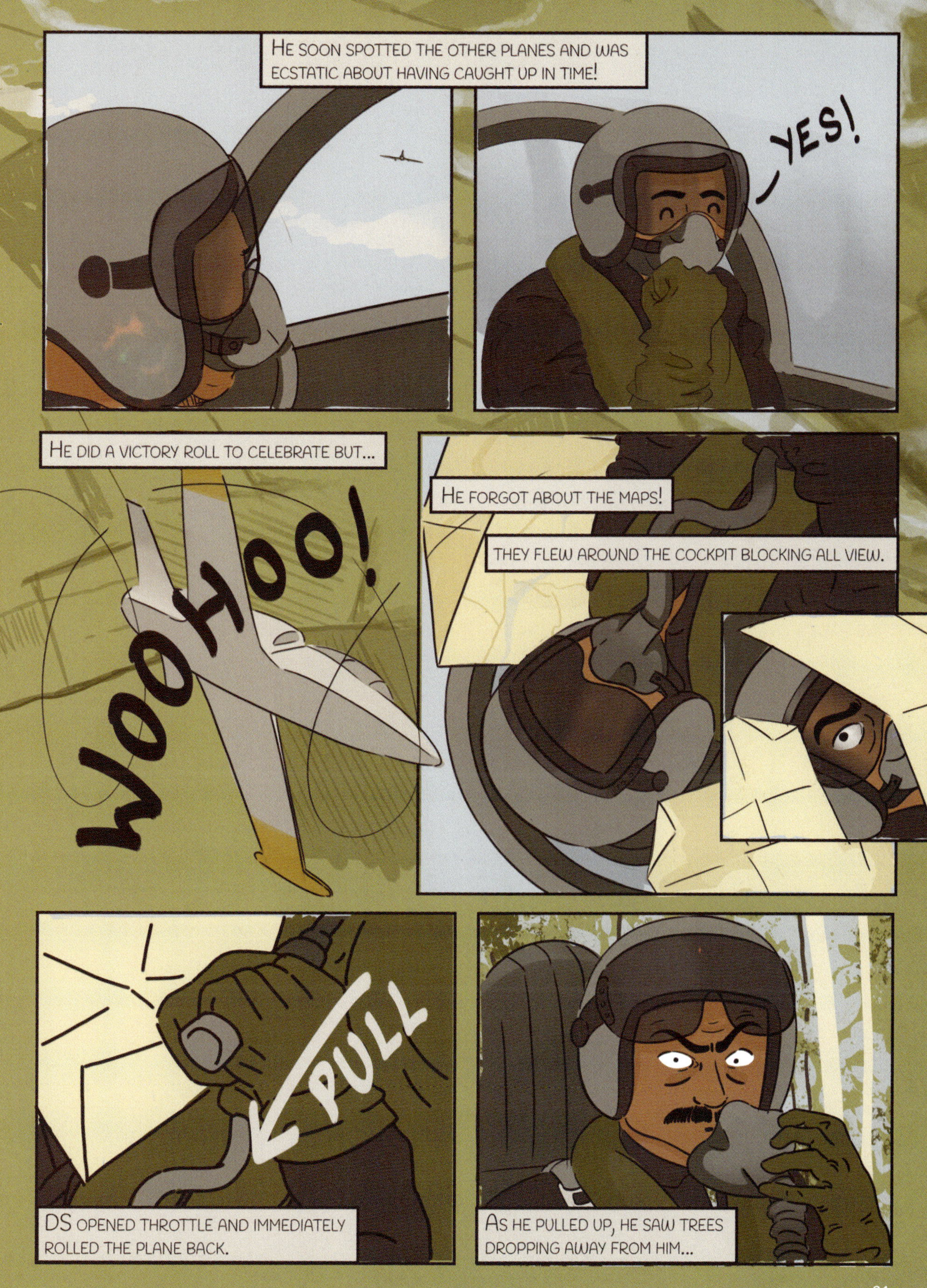
He soon spotted the other planes and was ecstatic about having caught up in time!
YES!
He did a victory roll to celebrate but...
WOOHOO!
He forgot about the maps!
They flew around the cockpit blocking all view.
PULL
DS opened throttle and immediately rolled the plane back.
As he pulled up, he saw trees dropping away from him...

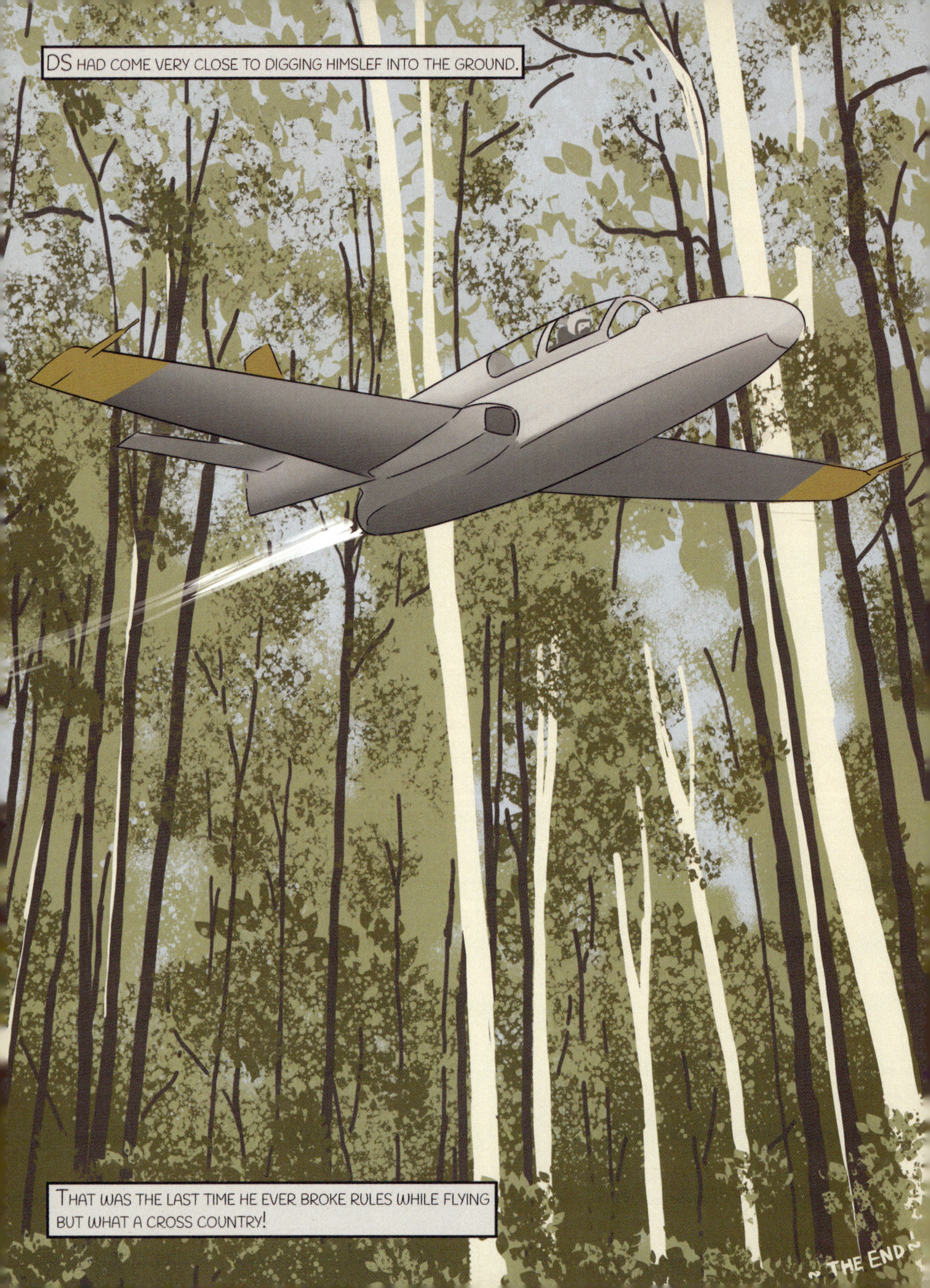
DS HAD COME VERY CLOSE TO DIGGING HIMSLEF INTO THE GROUND.
THAT WAS THE LAST TIME HE EVER BROKE RULES WHILE FLYING BUT WHAT A CROSS COUNTRY!
~ THE END ~

In conversation with Fighter Pilots #2

You've flown all over the country. What was your favourite terrain to fly in?

DS "Srinagar valley flying. Where else do you see the turquoise blue beauty of a mountain tarn resting in a hanging valley, nestled between ranks and ranks of emerald green pines."

Mukho "Desert flying! Can't tell which way is up and which is down. It's so hard to tell where the ground is because the rising and falling dunes just merge into each other. It's very exciting."

Sammy "Flying in the rain! Landing on a wet runway, the MiG 21 cleaves through water like a naval destroyer. The water goes up like 20ft in the air from the MiG 21 nose wheel."

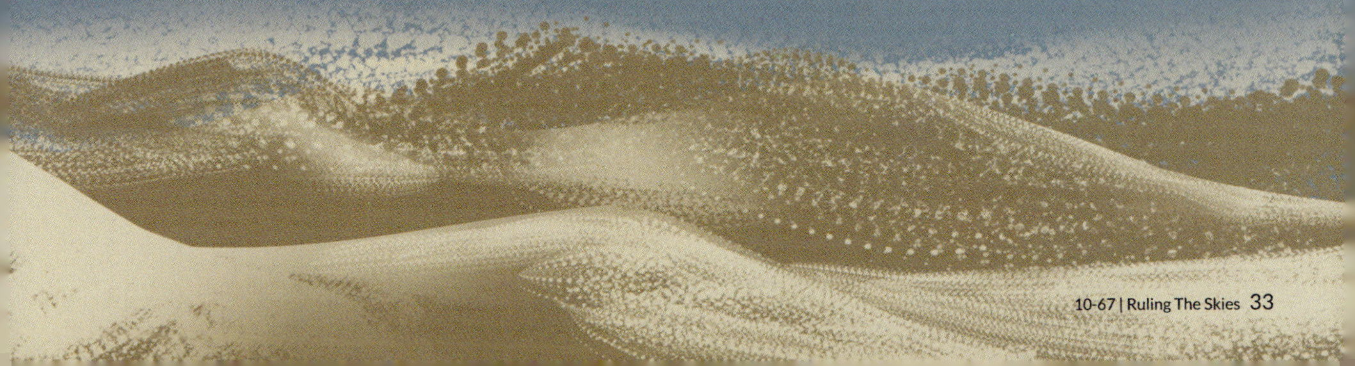

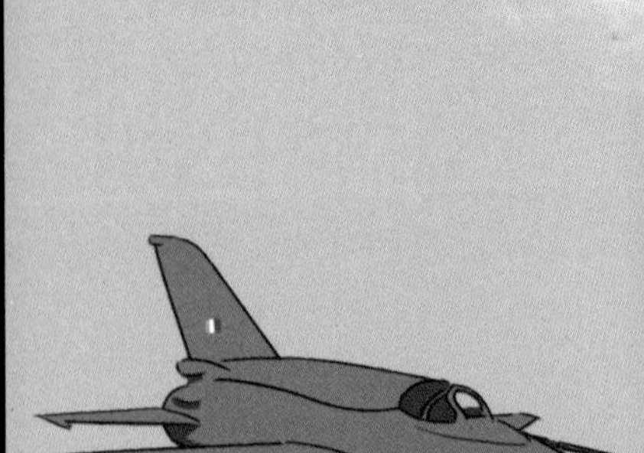

04

AN INVALID PASSPORT

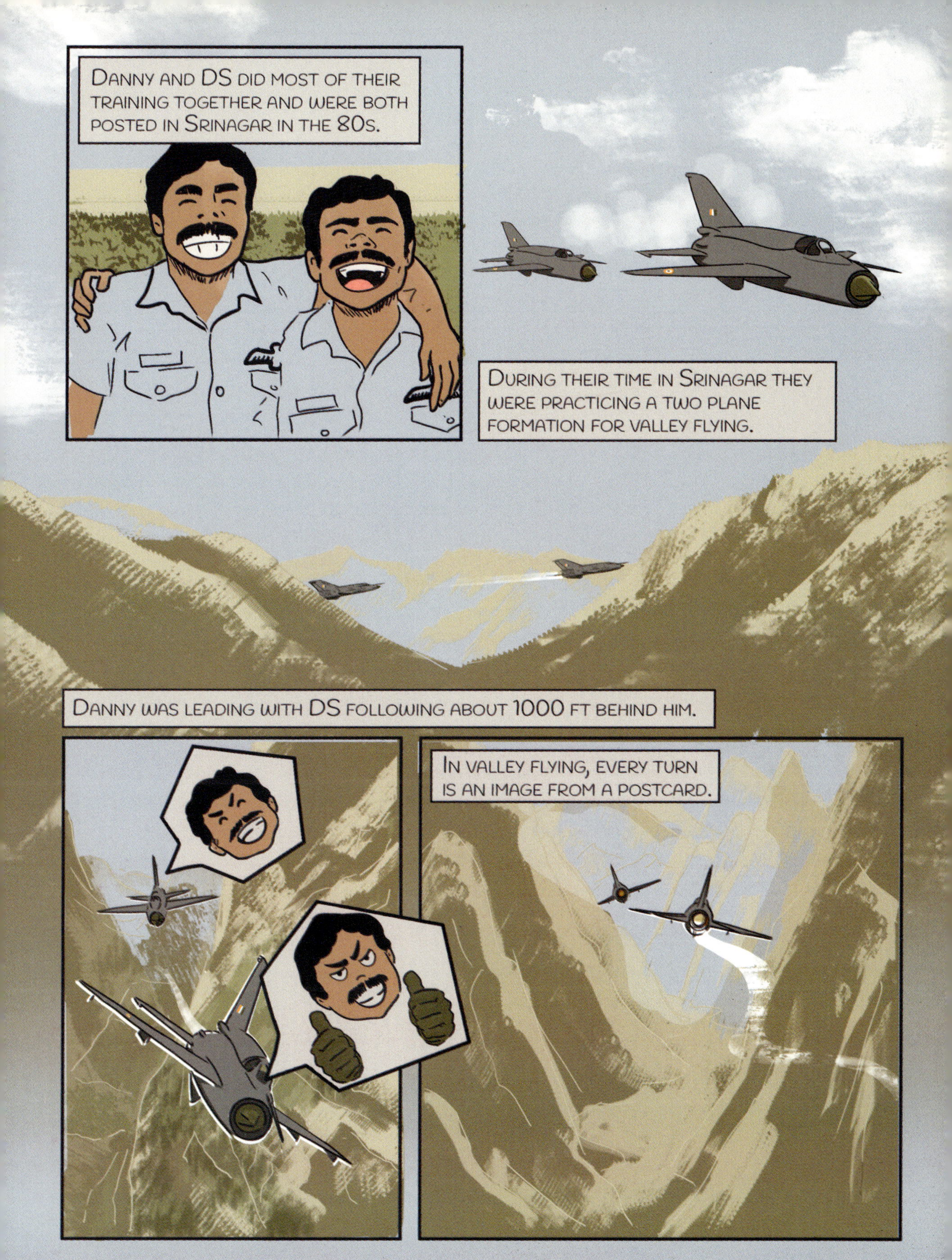
DANNY AND DS DID MOST OF THEIR TRAINING TOGETHER AND WERE BOTH POSTED IN SRINAGAR IN THE 80S.
DURING THEIR TIME IN SRINAGAR THEY WERE PRACTICING A TWO PLANE FORMATION FOR VALLEY FLYING.
DANNY WAS LEADING WITH DS FOLLOWING ABOUT 1000 FT BEHIND HIM.
IN VALLEY FLYING, EVERY TURN IS AN IMAGE FROM A POSTCARD.

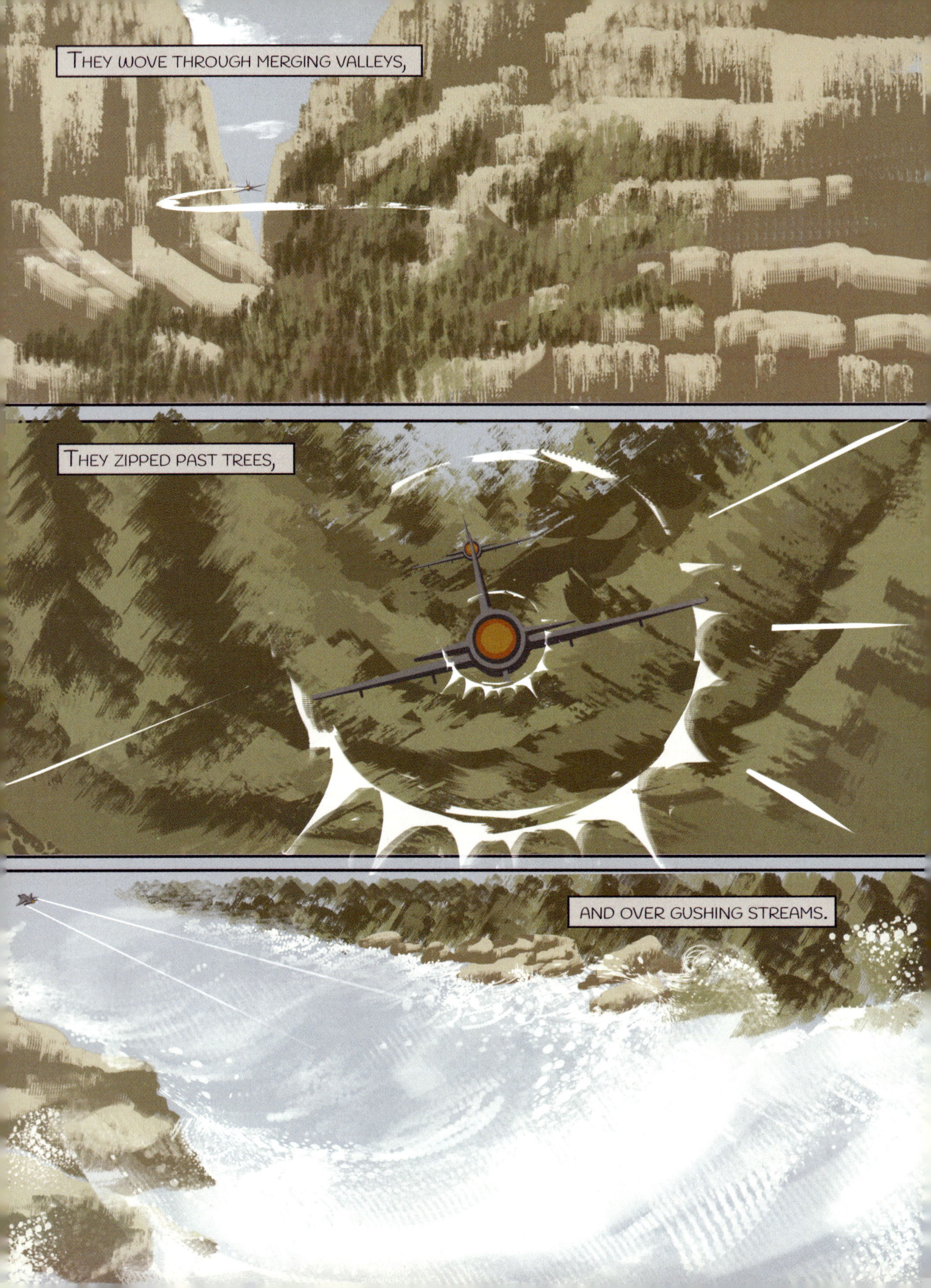
THEY WOVE THROUGH MERGING VALLEYS,
THEY ZIPPED PAST TREES,
AND OVER GUSHING STREAMS.

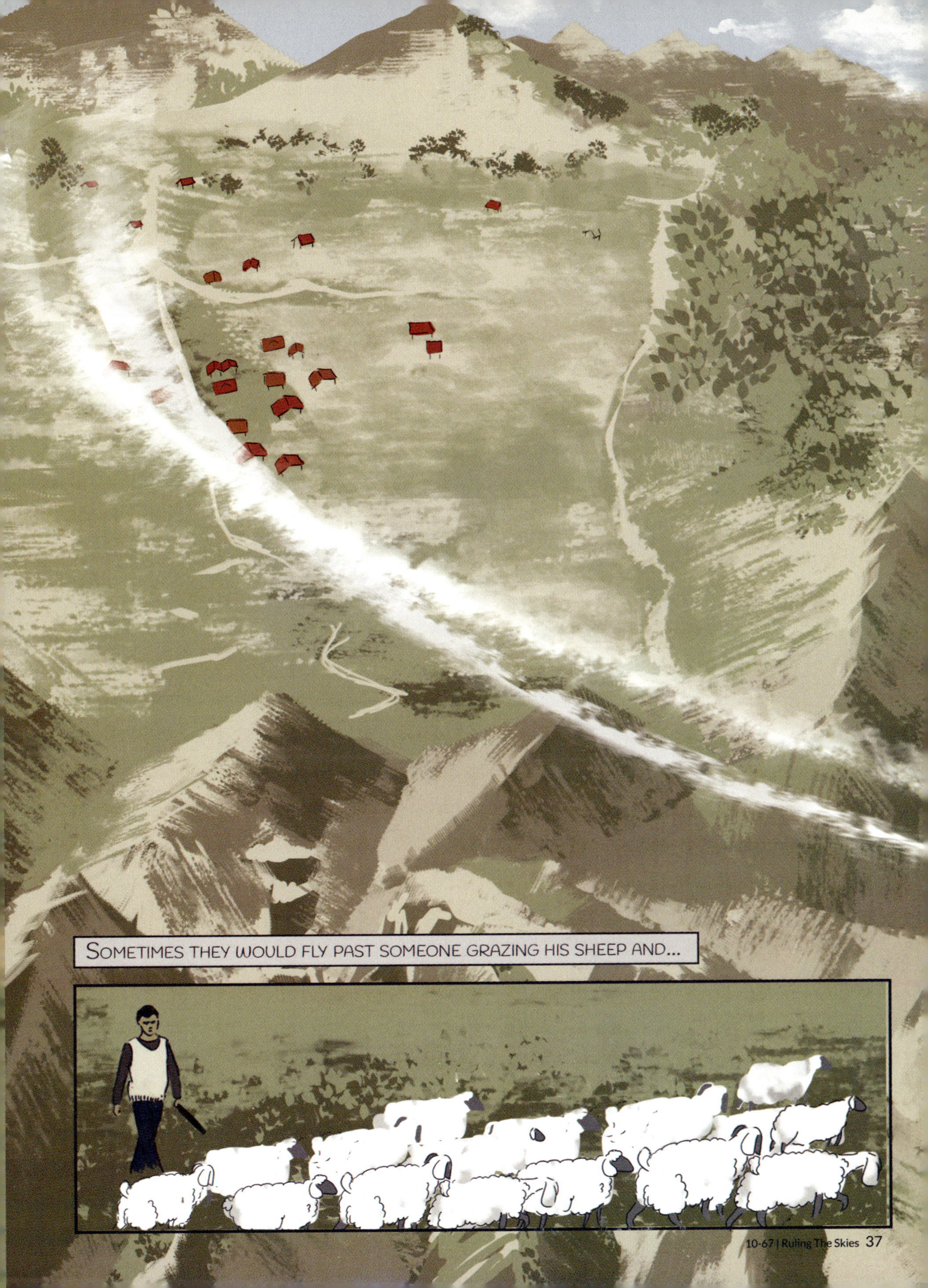
SOMETIMES THEY WOULD FLY PAST SOMEONE GRAZING HIS SHEEP AND...

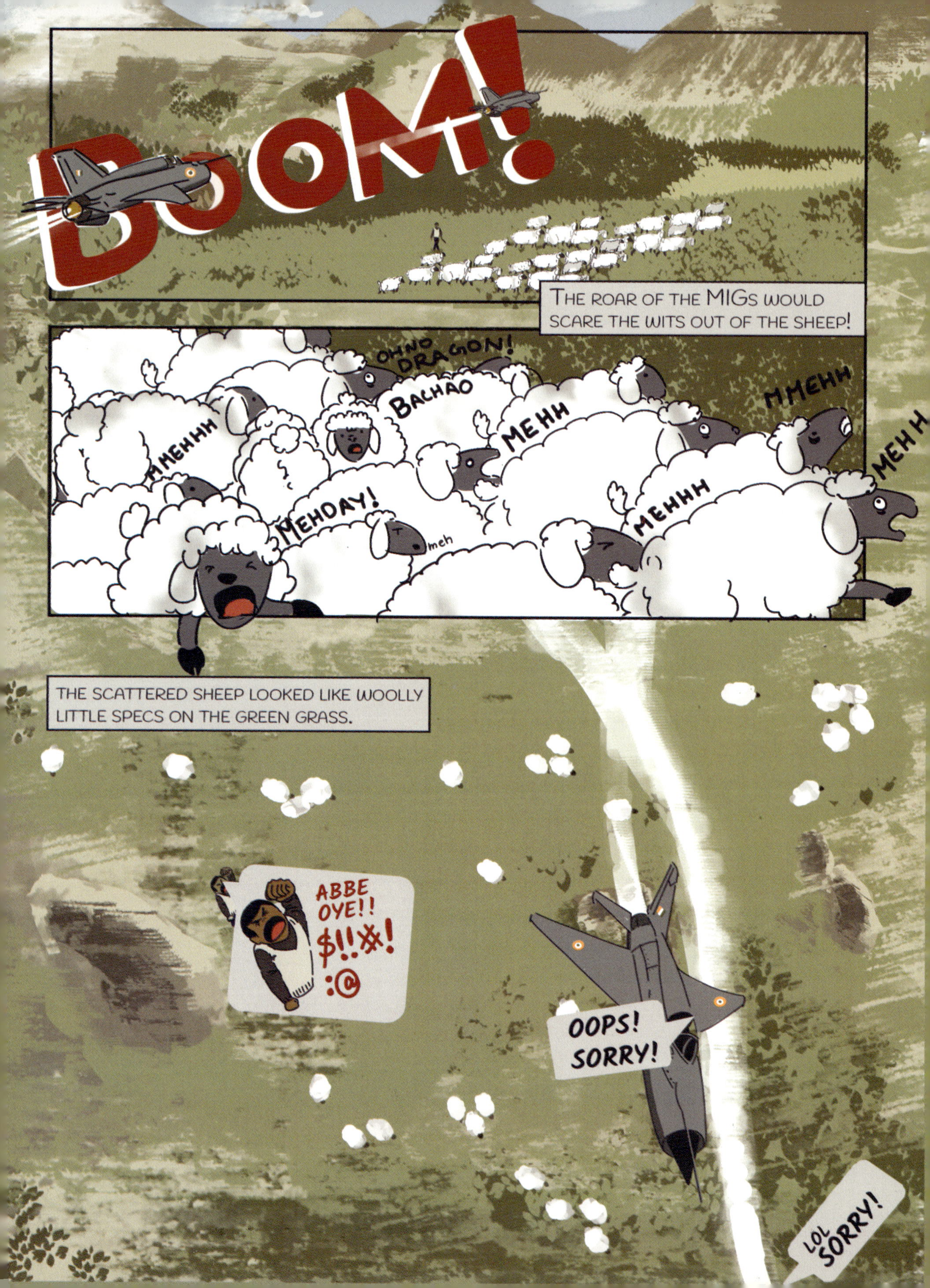
BOOM!
THE ROAR OF THE MIGS WOULD SCARE THE WITS OUT OF THE SHEEP!
OH NO DRAGON!
BACHAO
MMEHHH
MEHH
MMEHH
MEHH
MEHDAY!
meh
MEHHH
THE SCATTERED SHEEP LOOKED LIKE WOOLLY LITTLE SPECS ON THE GREEN GRASS.
ABBE OYE!! $!!*! :@
OOPS! SORRY!
LOL SORRY!

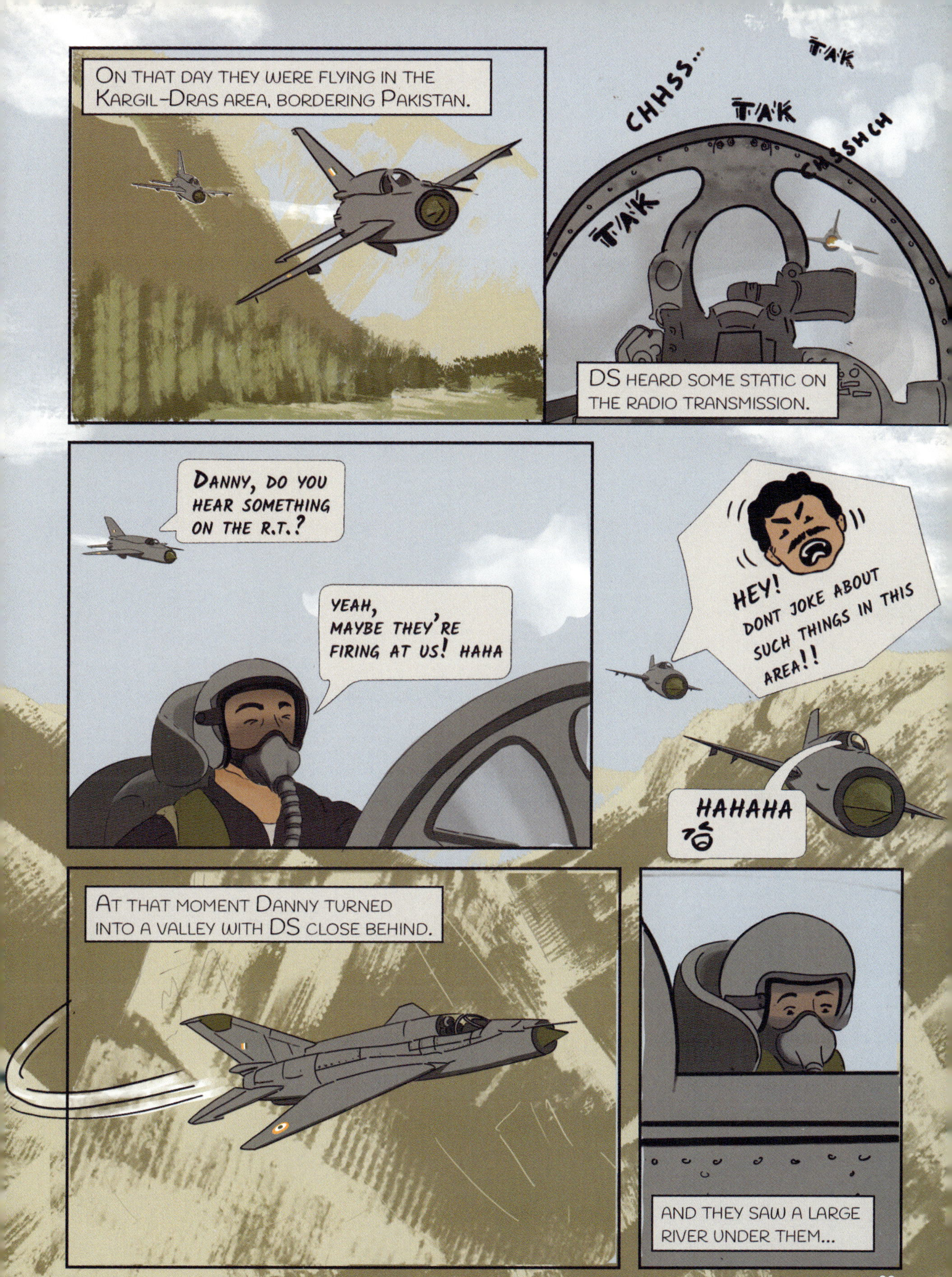

On that day they were flying in the Kargil–Dras area, bordering Pakistan.
CHHSS...
TA'K
TA'K
CHSSHCH
TA'K
DS heard some static on the radio transmission.
Danny, do you hear something on the R.T.?
Yeah, maybe they're firing at us! haha
Hey! Dont joke about such things in this area!!
HAHAHA
At that moment Danny turned into a valley with DS close behind.
And they saw a large river under them...

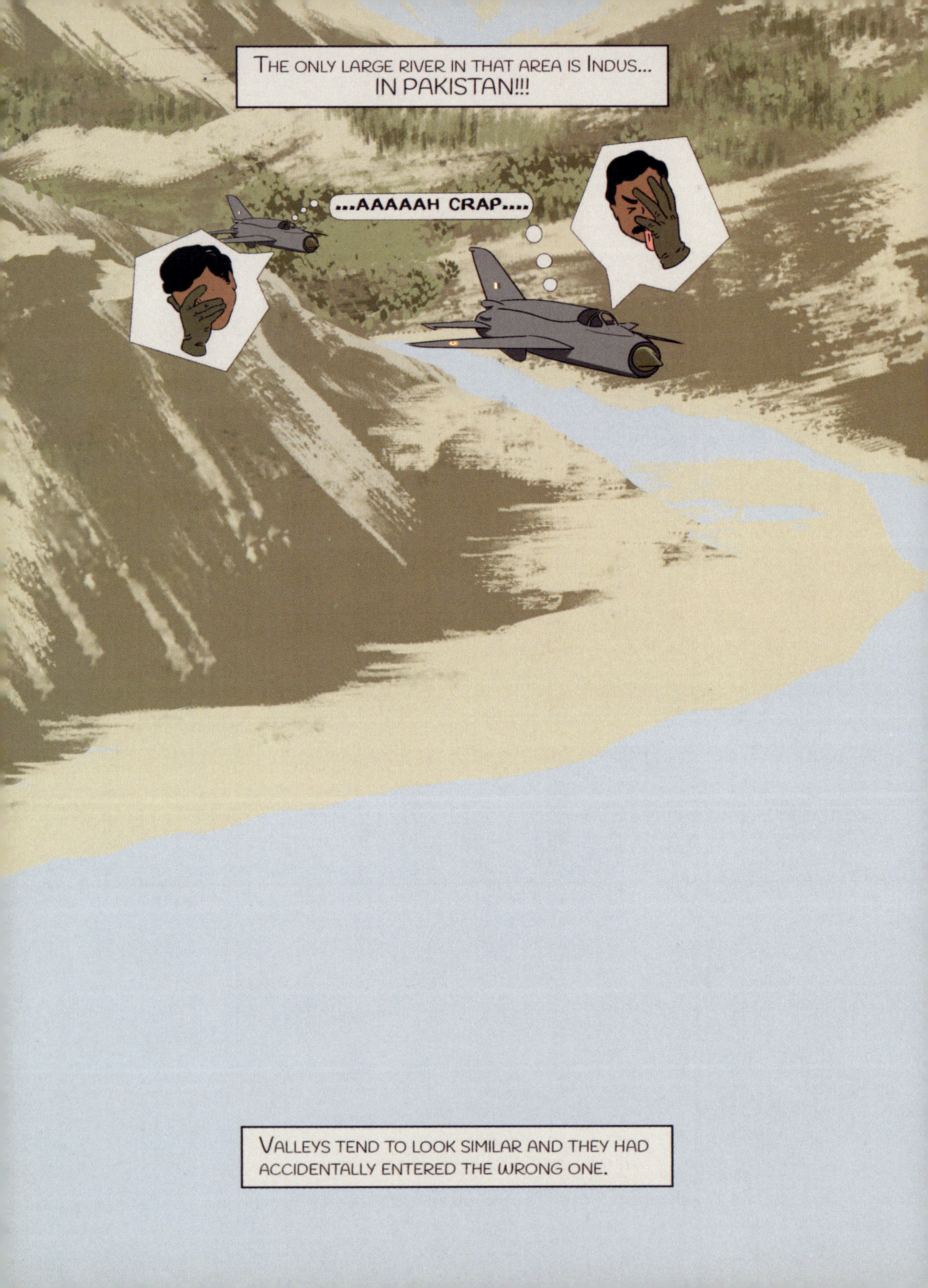
The only large river in that area is Indus...
IN PAKISTAN!!!
...AAAAAH CRAP....
Valleys tend to look similar and they had accidentally entered the wrong one.

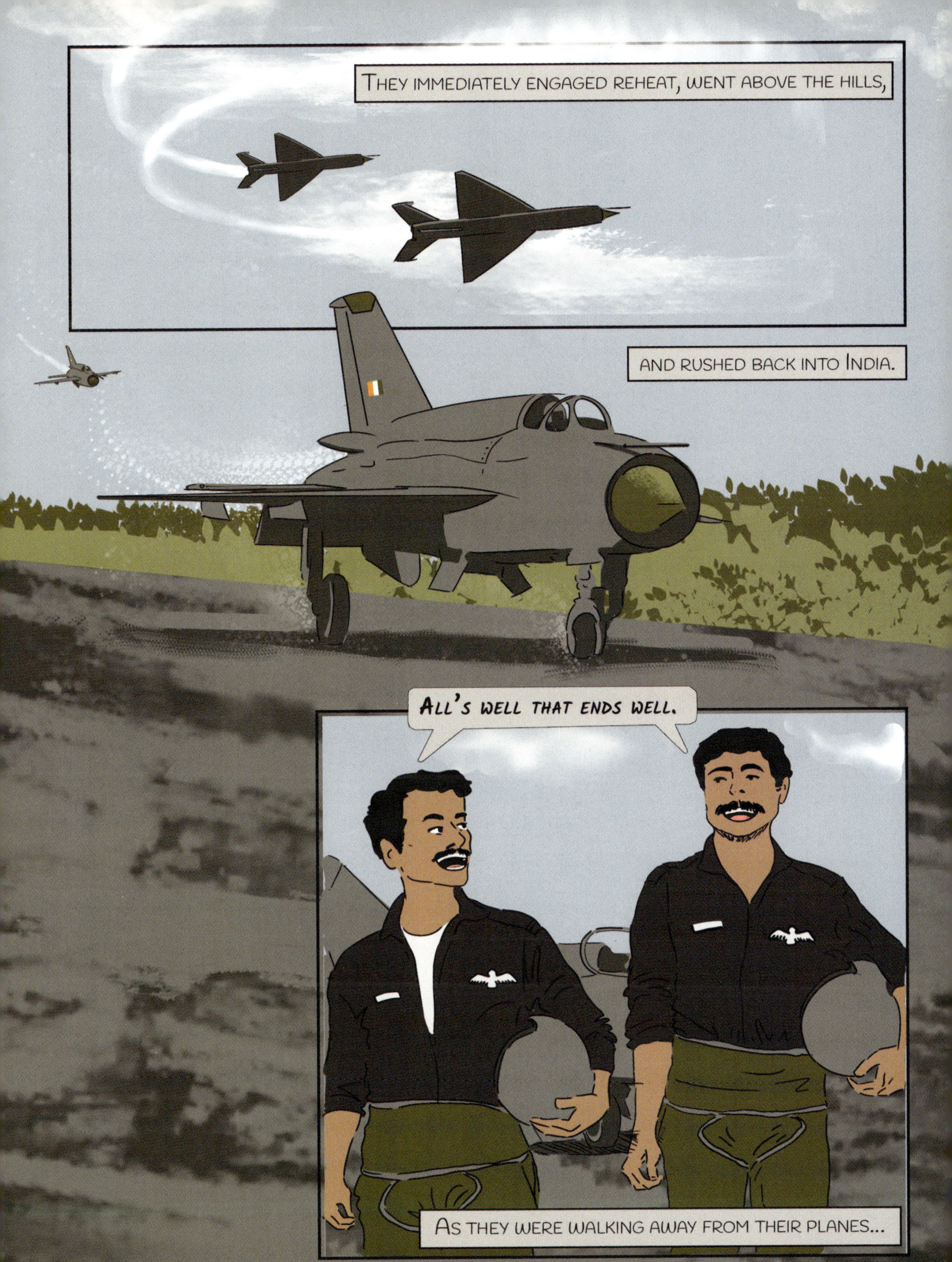
THEY IMMEDIATELY ENGAGED REHEAT, WENT ABOVE THE HILLS,
AND RUSHED BACK INTO INDIA.
ALL'S WELL THAT ENDS WELL.
AS THEY WERE WALKING AWAY FROM THEIR PLANES...

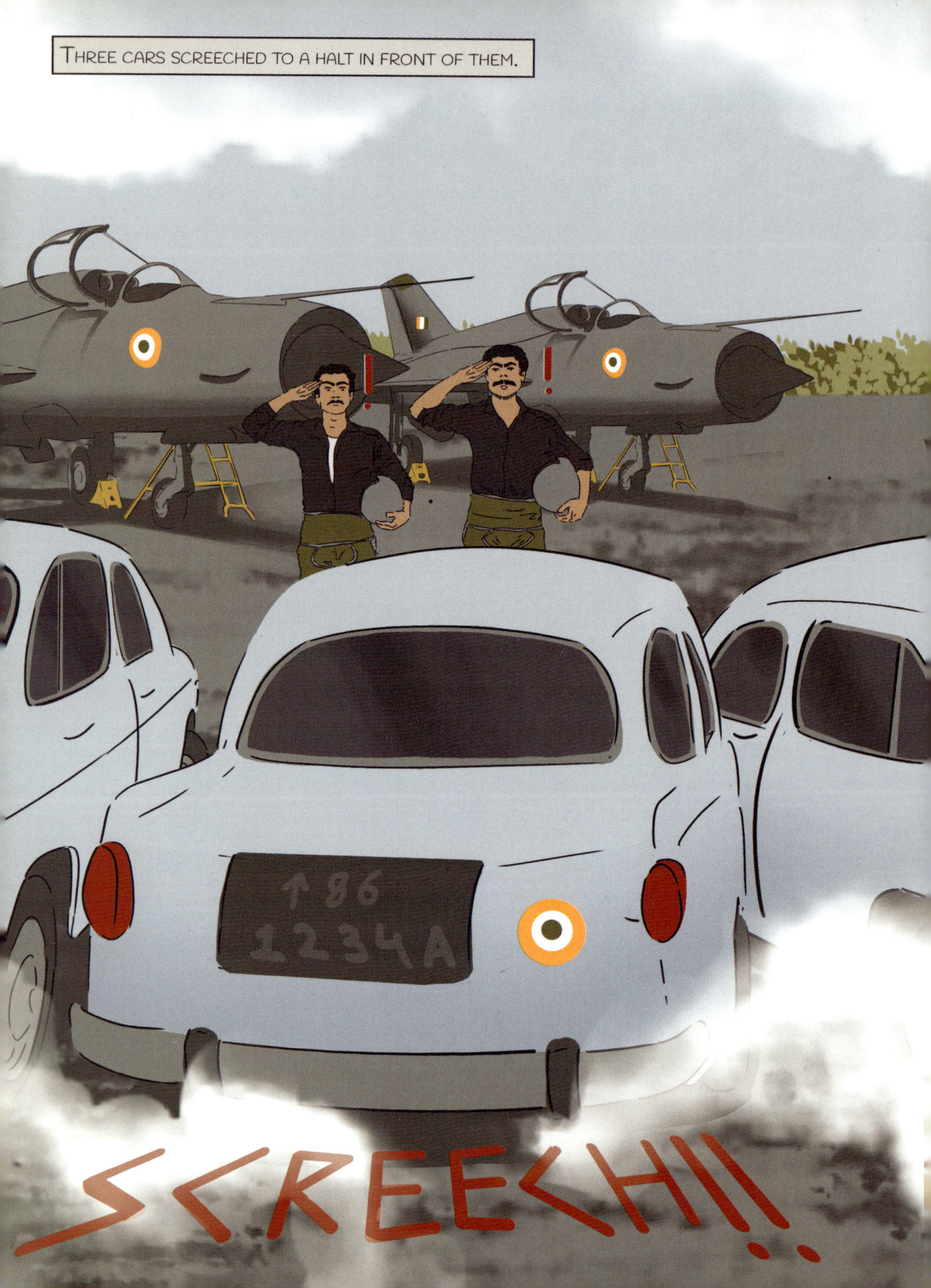
THREE CARS SCREECHED TO A HALT IN FRONT OF THEM.
↑86
1234A
SCREECH!!

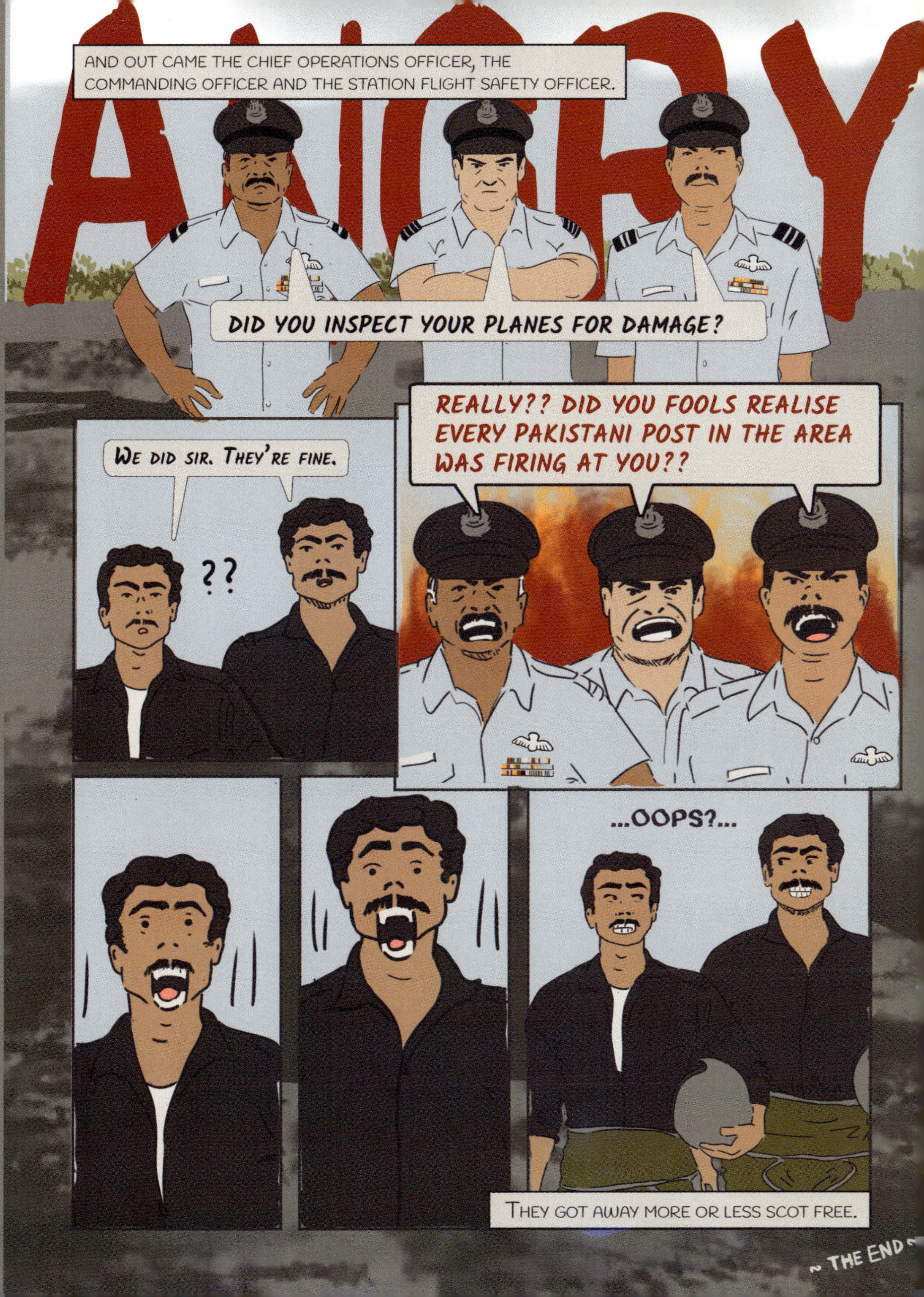
AND OUT CAME THE CHIEF OPERATIONS OFFICER, THE COMMANDING OFFICER AND THE STATION FLIGHT SAFETY OFFICER.
DID YOU INSPECT YOUR PLANES FOR DAMAGE?
WE DID SIR. THEY'RE FINE.
??
REALLY?? DID YOU FOOLS REALISE EVERY PAKISTANI POST IN THE AREA WAS FIRING AT YOU??
...OOPS?...
THEY GOT AWAY MORE OR LESS SCOT FREE.
~ THE END ~

05

SLOW AND STEADY

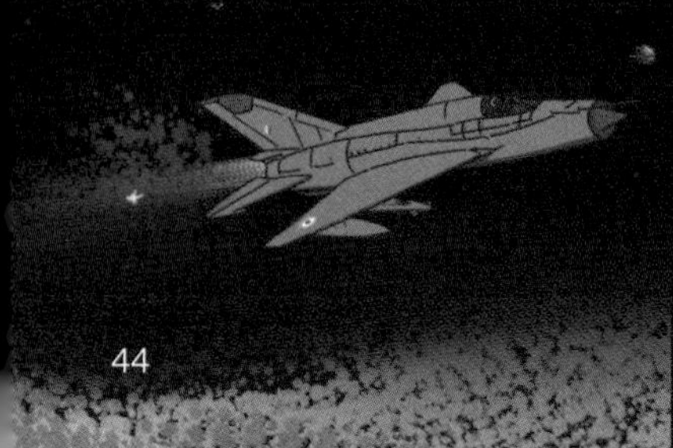

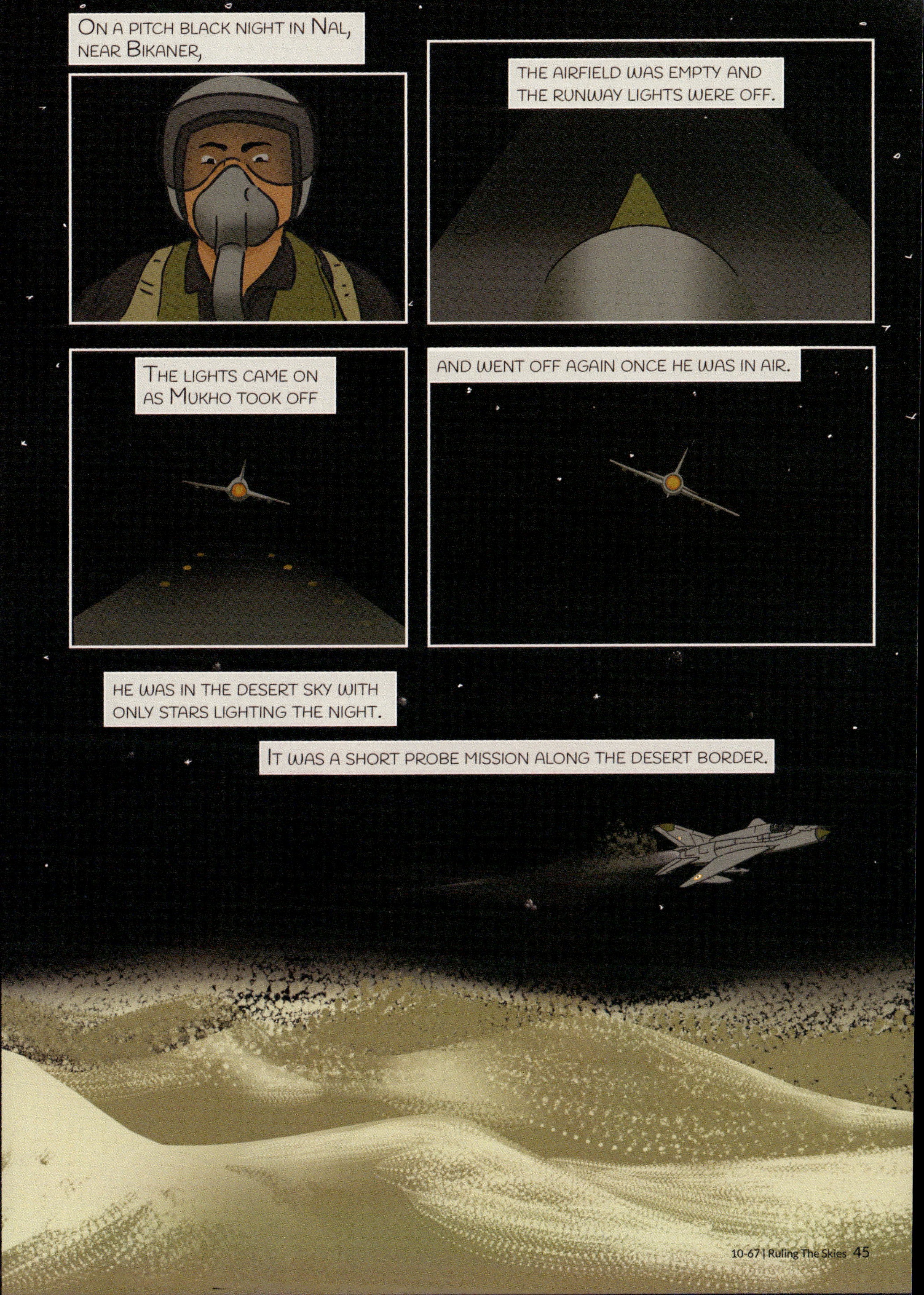
On a pitch black night in Nal, near Bikaner,
The airfield was empty and the runway lights were off.
The lights came on as Mukho took off
and went off again once he was in air.
He was in the desert sky with only stars lighting the night.
It was a short probe mission along the desert border.

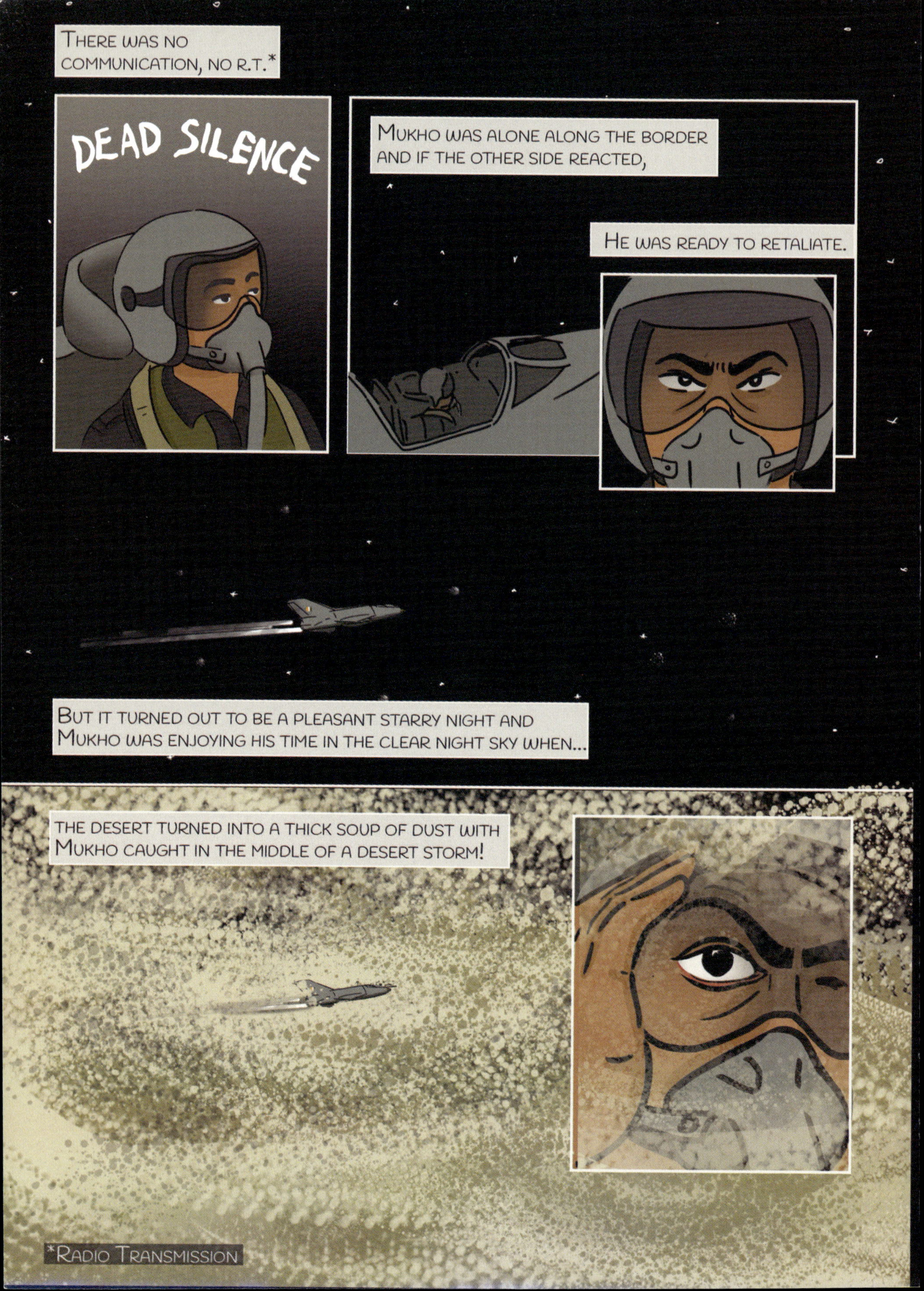
There was no communication, no R.T.*
DEAD SILENCE
Mukho was alone along the border and if the other side reacted,
He was ready to retaliate.
But it turned out to be a pleasant starry night and Mukho was enjoying his time in the clear night sky when...
The desert turned into a thick soup of dust with Mukho caught in the middle of a desert storm!
*Radio Transmission

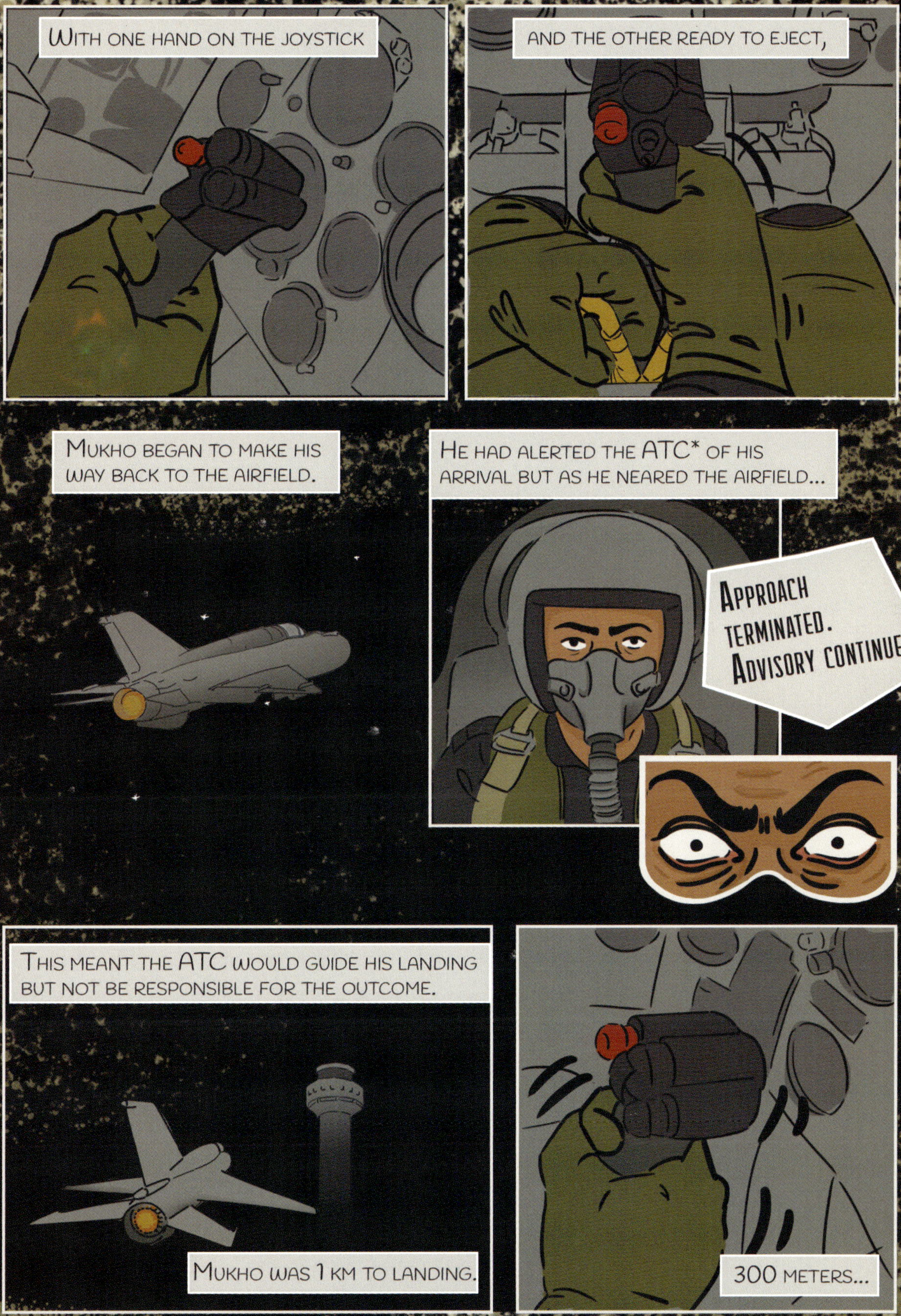

* AIR TRAFFIC CONTROL

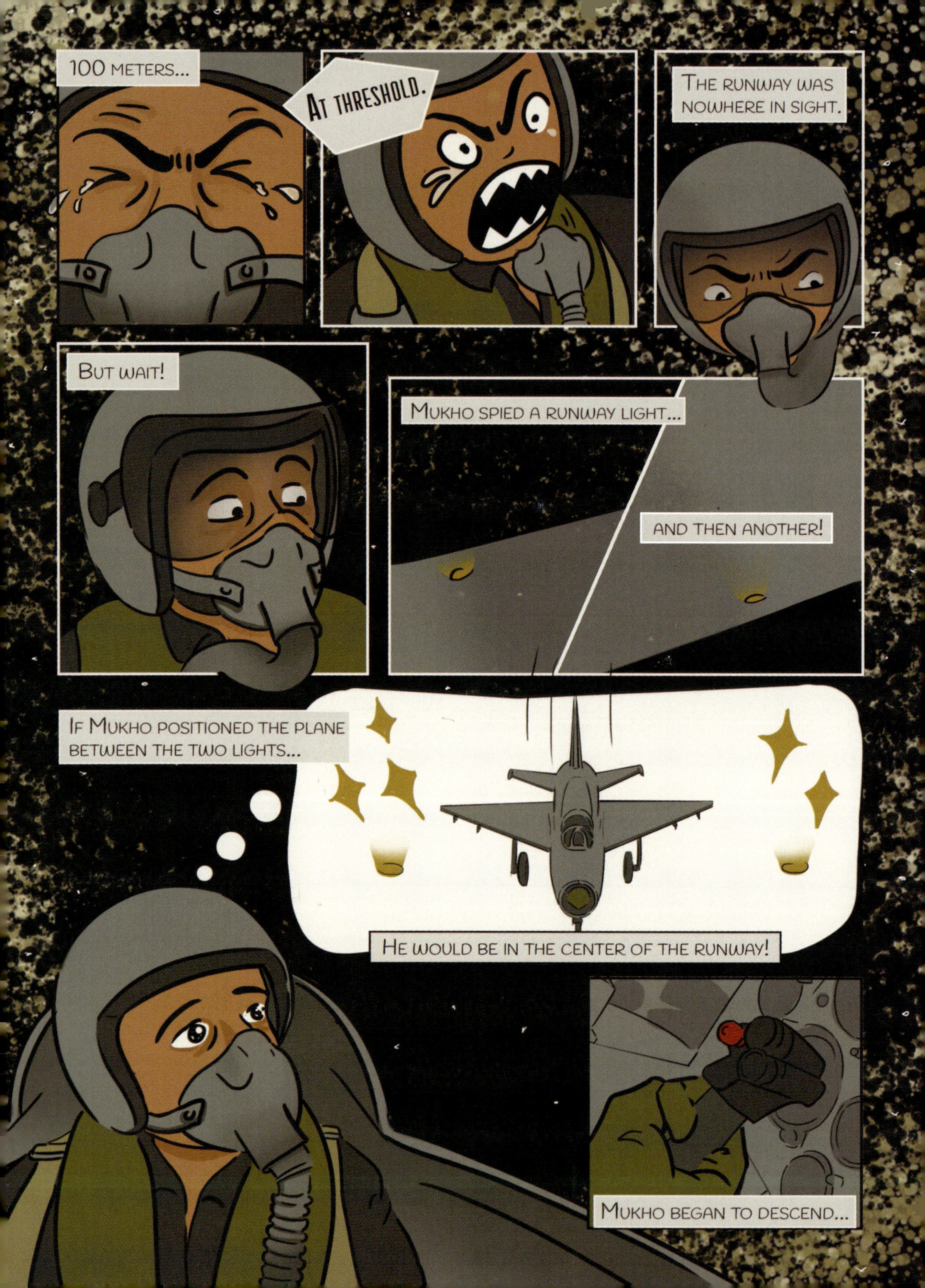
100 METERS...
AT THRESHOLD.
THE RUNWAY WAS NOWHERE IN SIGHT.
BUT WAIT!
MUKHO SPIED A RUNWAY LIGHT...
AND THEN ANOTHER!
IF MUKHO POSITIONED THE PLANE BETWEEN THE TWO LIGHTS...
HE WOULD BE IN THE CENTER OF THE RUNWAY!
MUKHO BEGAN TO DESCEND...

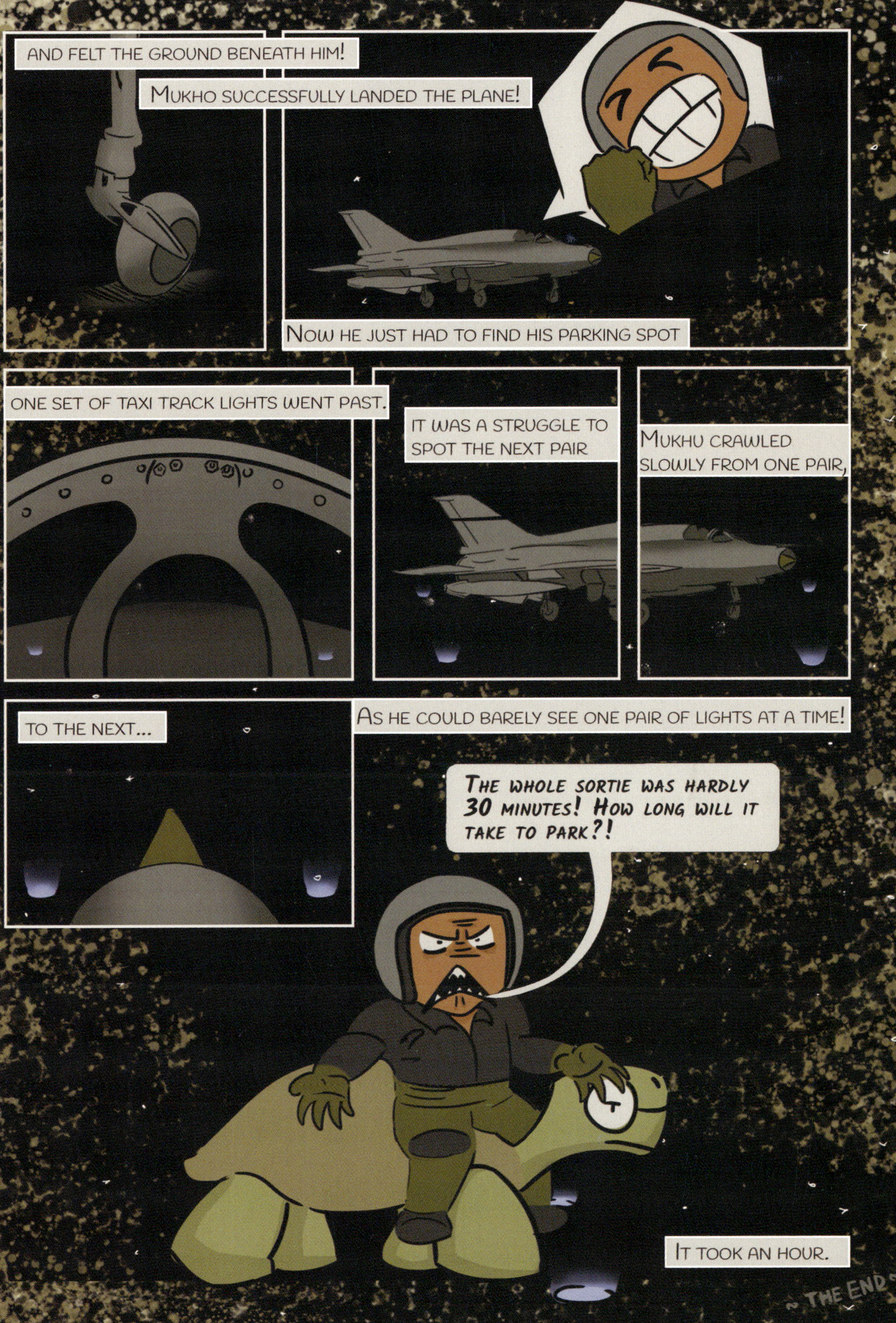

AND FELT THE GROUND BENEATH HIM!
MUKHO SUCCESSFULLY LANDED THE PLANE!
NOW HE JUST HAD TO FIND HIS PARKING SPOT
ONE SET OF TAXI TRACK LIGHTS WENT PAST.
IT WAS A STRUGGLE TO SPOT THE NEXT PAIR
MUKHU CRAWLED SLOWLY FROM ONE PAIR,
TO THE NEXT...
AS HE COULD BARELY SEE ONE PAIR OF LIGHTS AT A TIME!
THE WHOLE SORTIE WAS HARDLY 30 MINUTES! HOW LONG WILL IT TAKE TO PARK?!
IT TOOK AN HOUR.
~ THE END ~

06

A SMALL FAVOUR

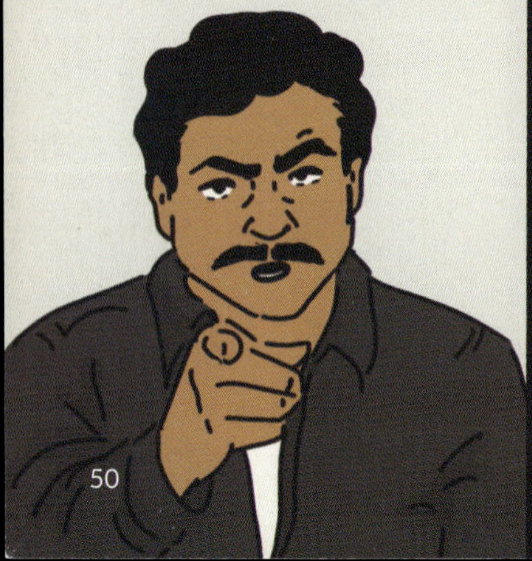

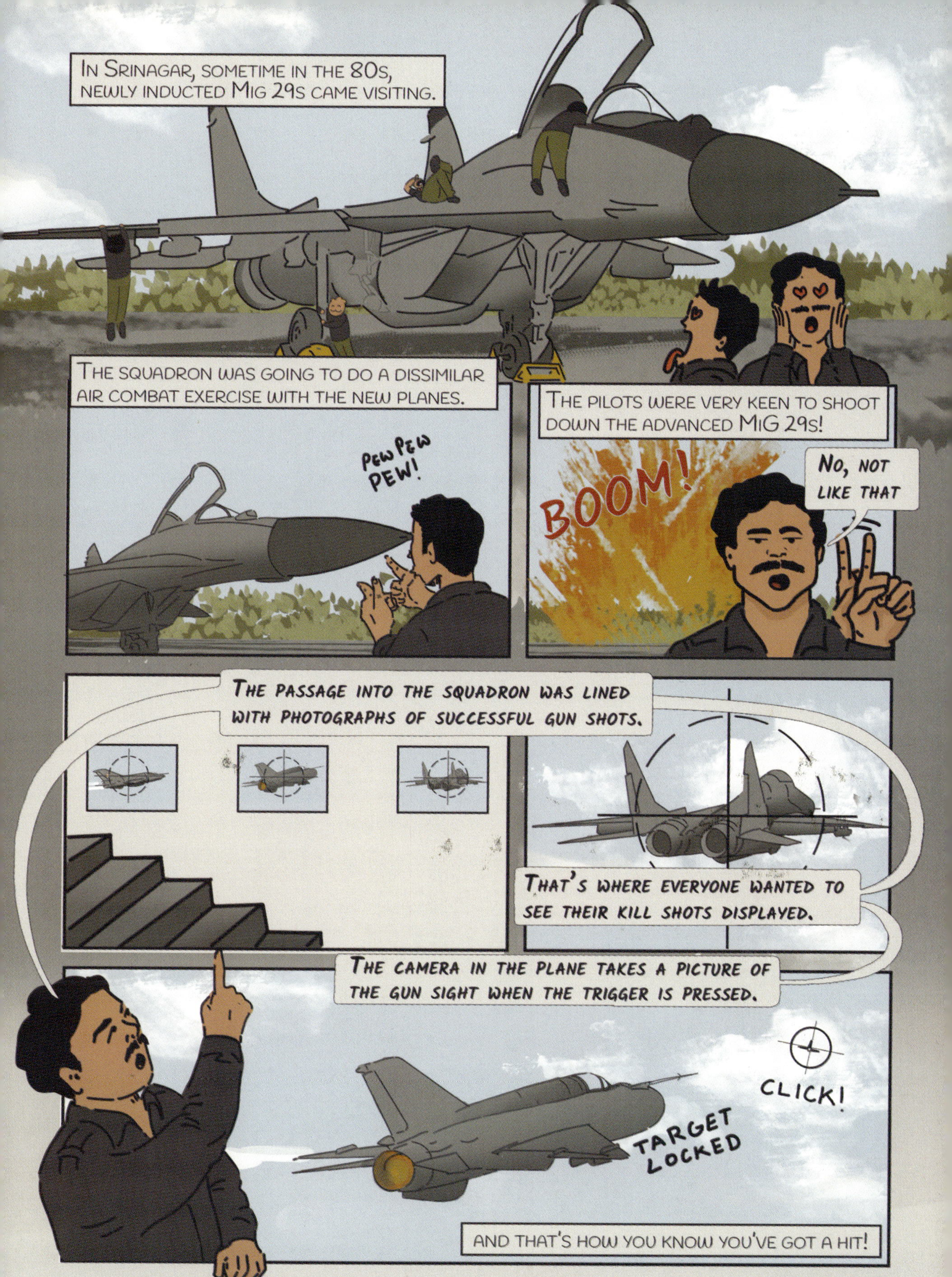
In Srinagar, sometime in the 80s, newly inducted MiG 29s came visiting.
The squadron was going to do a dissimilar air combat exercise with the new planes.
Pew Pew PEW!
The pilots were very keen to shoot down the advanced MiG 29s!
BOOM!
No, not like that
The passage into the squadron was lined with photographs of successful gun shots.
That's where everyone wanted to see their kill shots displayed.
The camera in the plane takes a picture of the gun sight when the trigger is pressed.
CLICK!
TARGET LOCKED
And that's how you know you've got a hit!

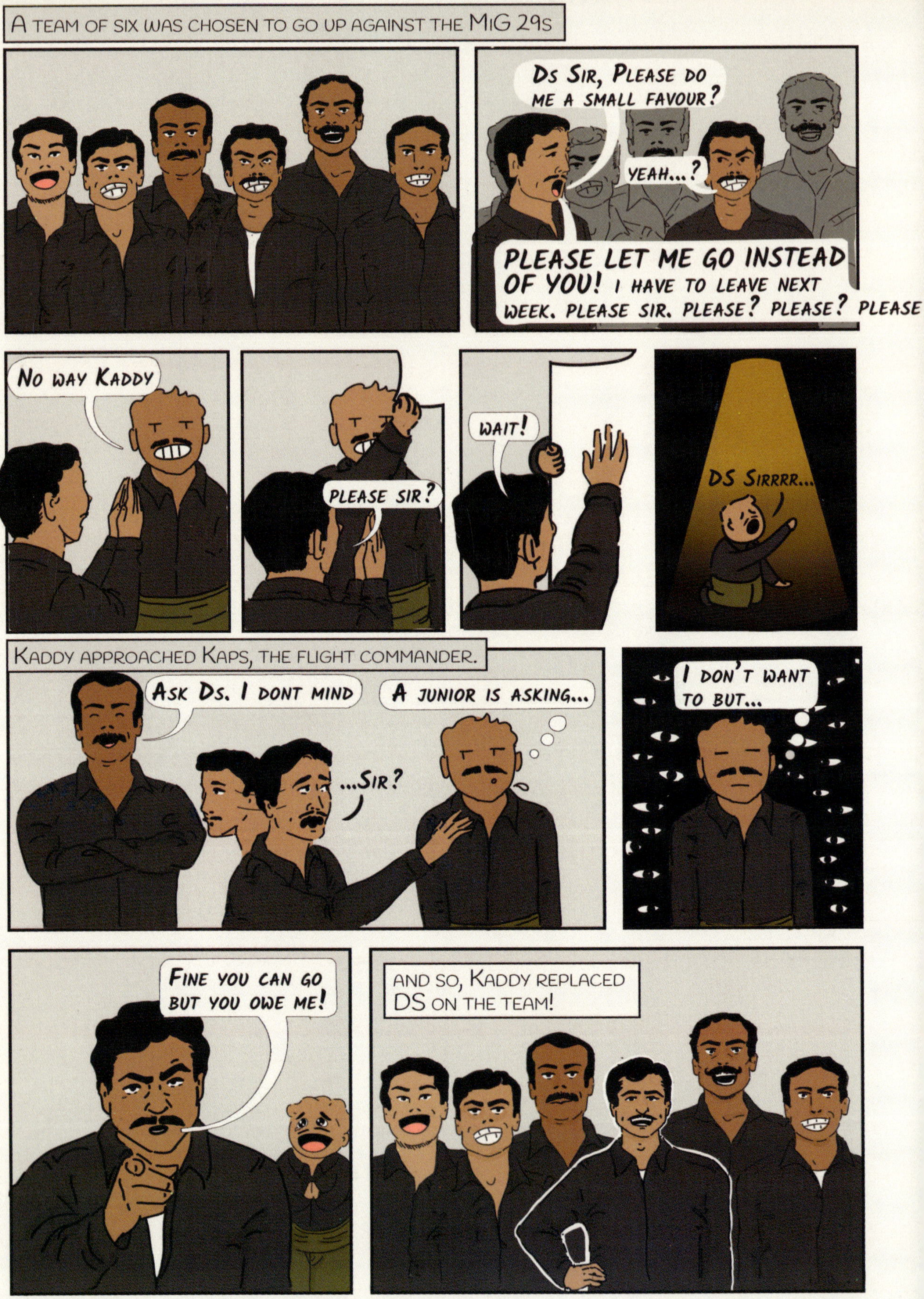
A TEAM OF SIX WAS CHOSEN TO GO UP AGAINST THE MiG 29s
Ds Sir, Please do me a small favour?
Yeah...?
PLEASE LET ME GO INSTEAD OF YOU! I HAVE TO LEAVE NEXT WEEK. PLEASE SIR. PLEASE? PLEASE? PLEASE
No way Kaddy
Please sir?
Wait!
DS Sirrrr...
Kaddy approached Kaps, the flight commander.
Ask Ds. I dont mind
A junior is asking...
...Sir?
I don't want to but...
Fine you can go but you owe me!
And so, Kaddy replaced DS on the team!

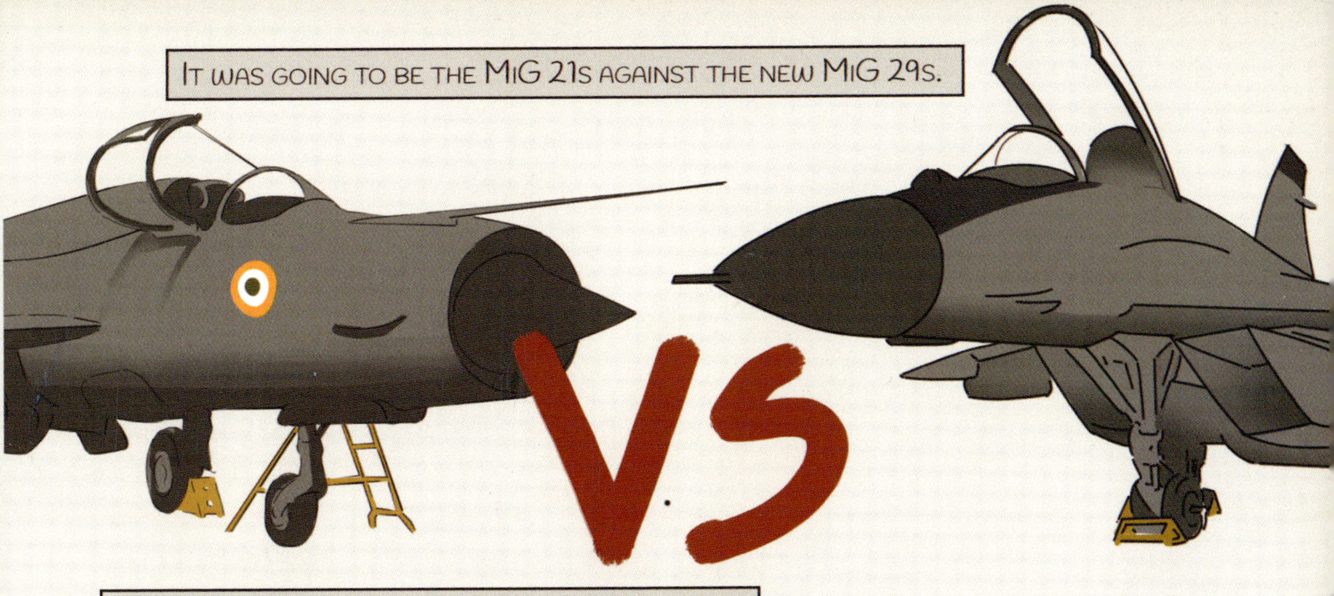
It was going to be the MiG 21s against the new MiG 29s.
VS

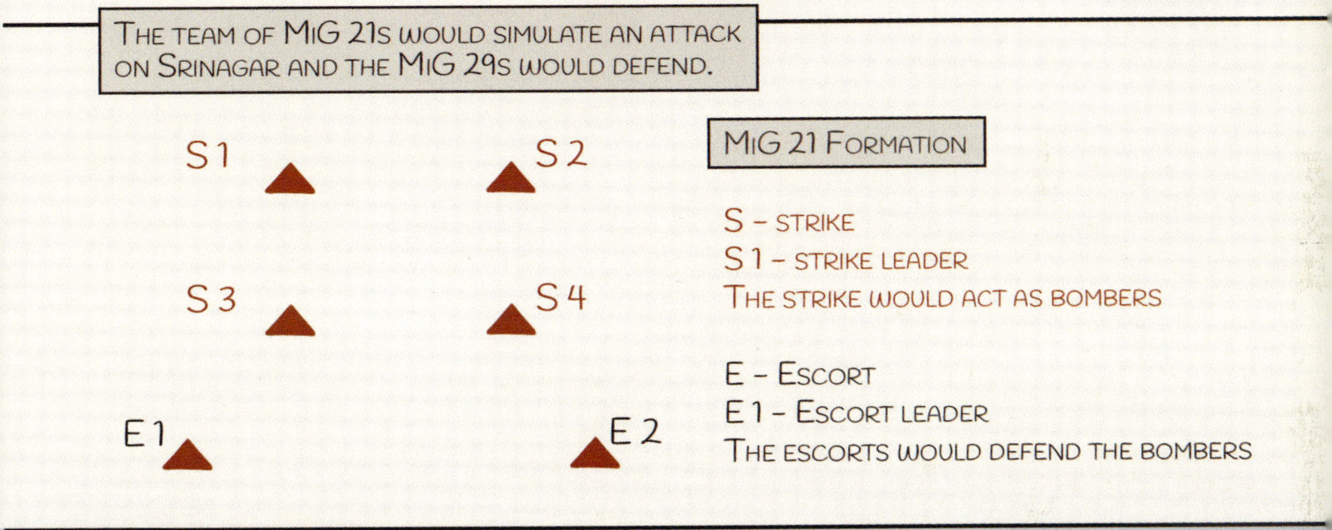
The team of MiG 21s would simulate an attack on Srinagar and the MiG 29s would defend.
S1
S2
S3
S4
E1
E2
MiG 21 Formation
S – strike
S1 – strike leader
The strike would act as bombers
E – Escort
E1 – Escort leader
The escorts would defend the bombers

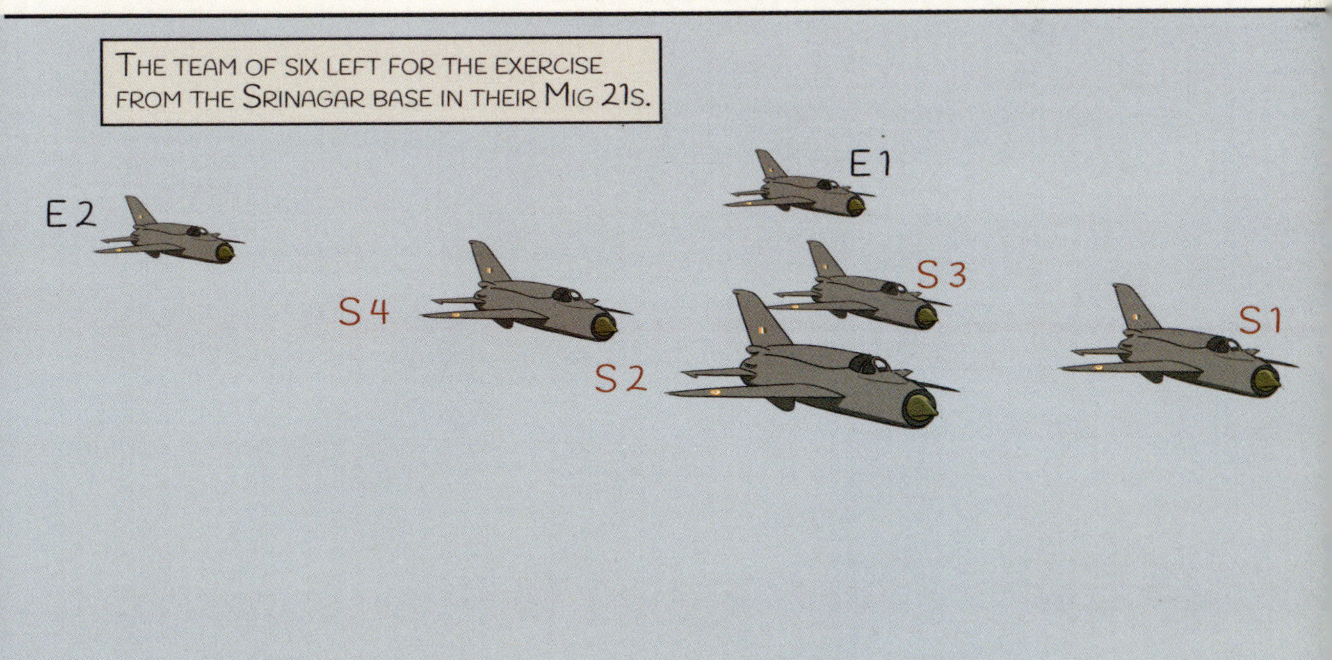
The team of six left for the exercise from the Srinagar base in their Mig 21s.
E1
E2
S3
S4
S1
S2

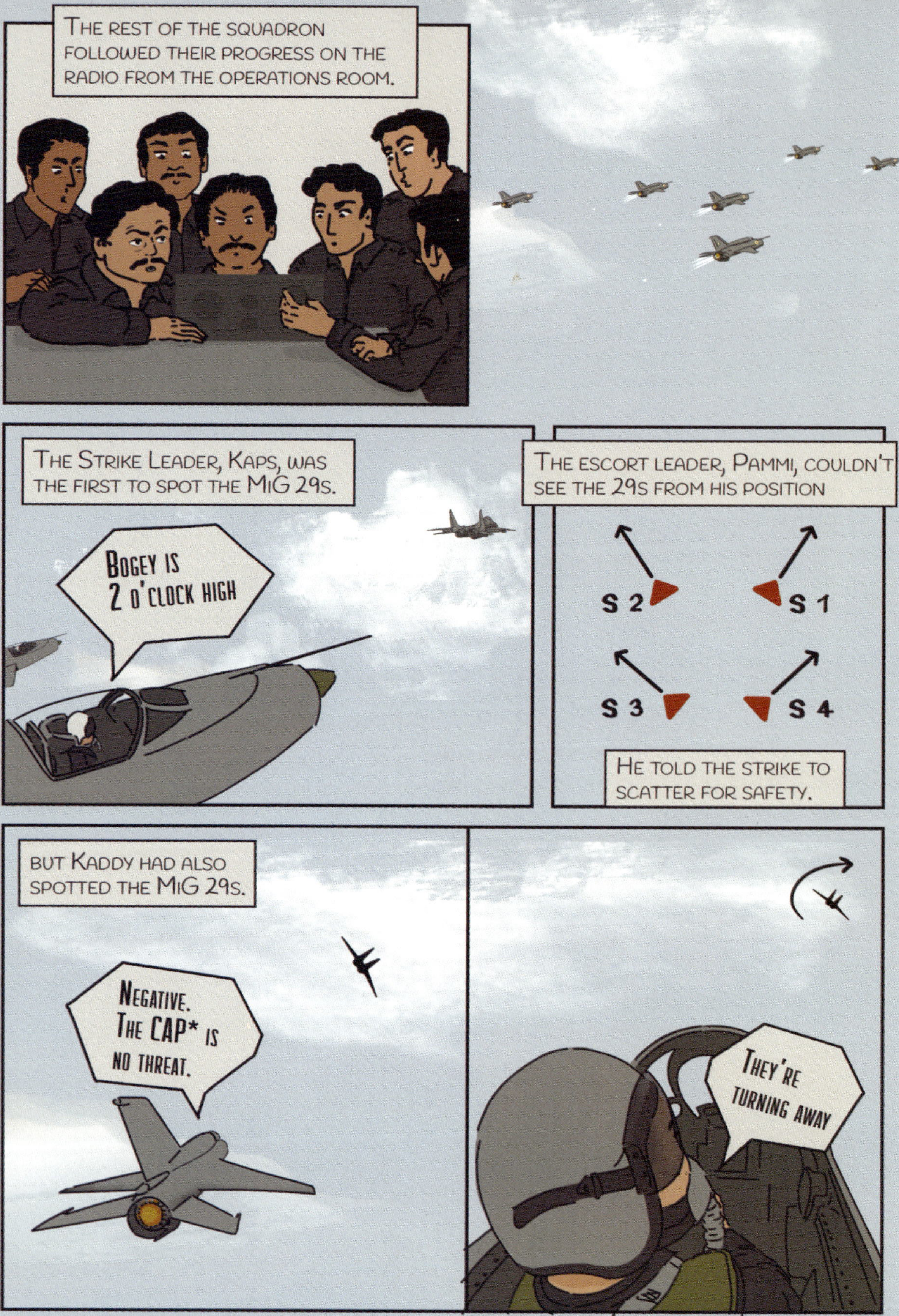

*COMBAT AIR PATROL. HE'S REFERING TO THE MIG 29S PATROLLING THE SKIES FOR ENEMY MIG 21S

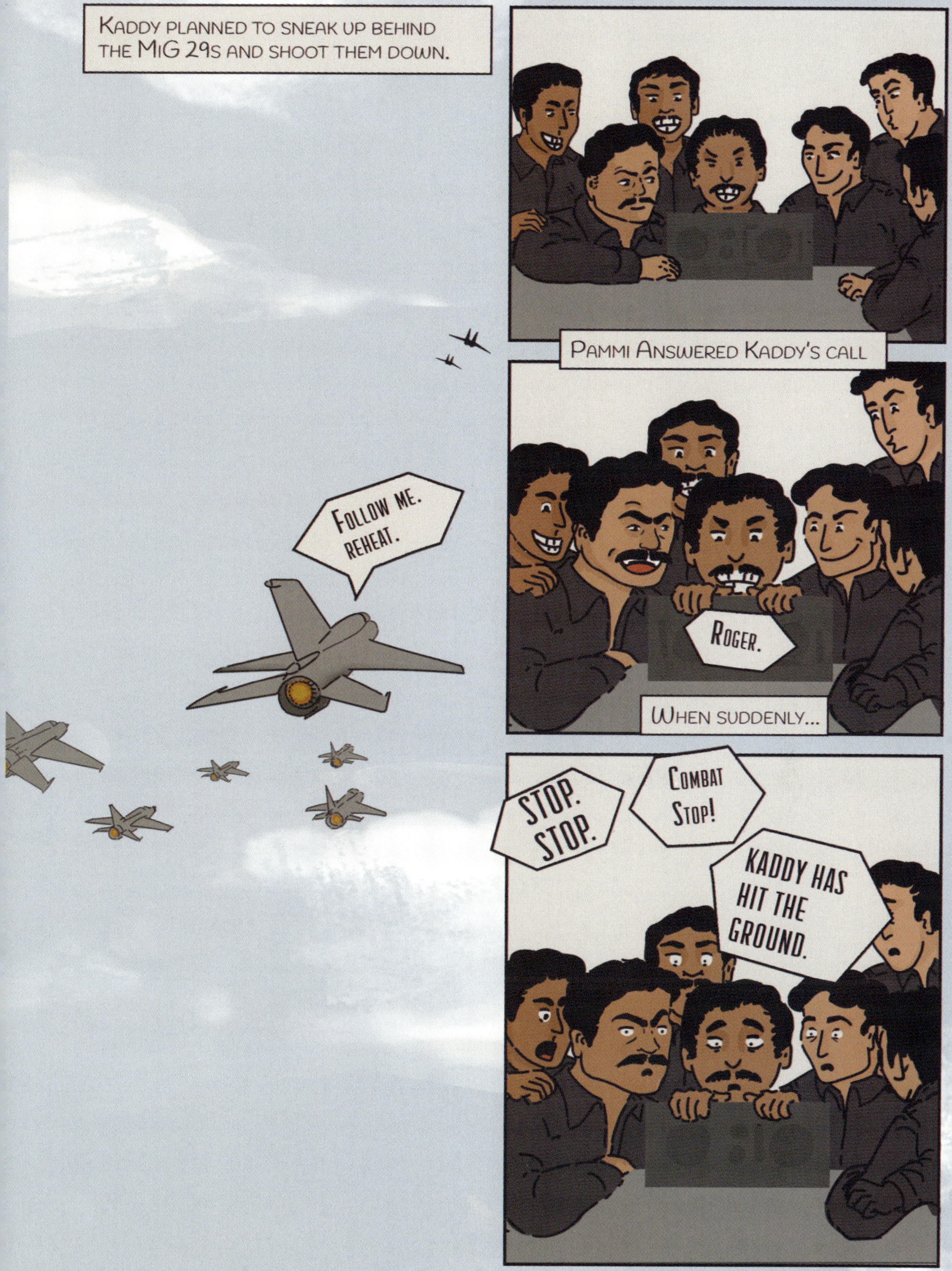
KADDY PLANNED TO SNEAK UP BEHIND THE MiG 29S AND SHOOT THEM DOWN.
PAMMI ANSWERED KADDY'S CALL
FOLLOW ME. REHEAT.
ROGER.
WHEN SUDDENLY...
STOP. STOP.
COMBAT STOP!
KADDY HAS HIT THE GROUND.

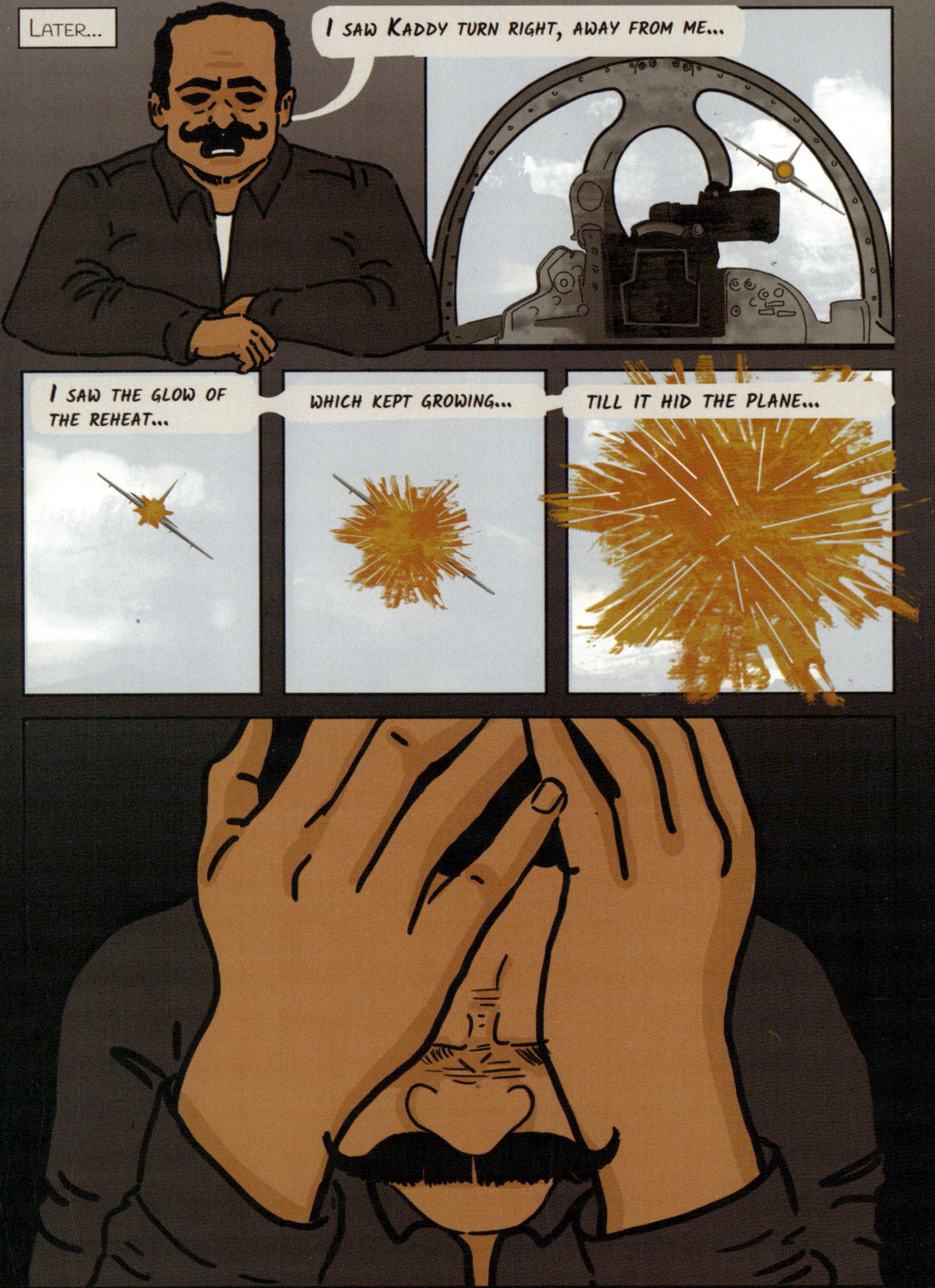
LATER...
I SAW KADDY TURN RIGHT, AWAY FROM ME...
I SAW THE GLOW OF THE REHEAT...
WHICH KEPT GROWING...
TILL IT HID THE PLANE...

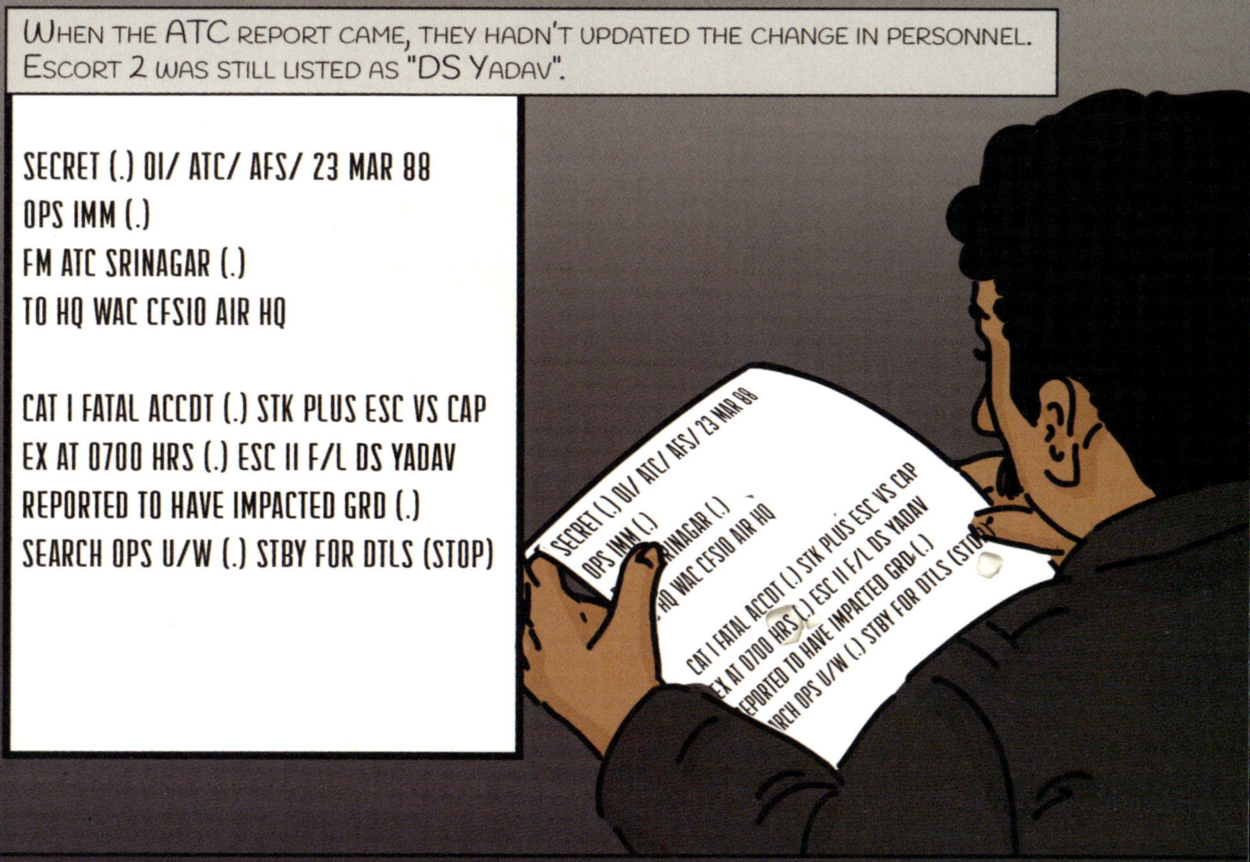

When the inquiry report came in, they found that something had gone wrong with the reheat system and the aircraft was suddenly gaining 10s of km of speed per second. It basically became like a rocket. Kaddy took the correct actions and immediately tried to close throttle. He pulled out his speed breaks but the plane had gone past supersonic speed and hit the ground. He was a good pilot and a dear friend to his colleagues.

All the pilots I spoke to were well aware of the dangers in fighter flying though many attributed fatal accidents to lack of experience and human errors. When I questioned them about the concerns that have been raised about MiG 21s, many said you have to know this plane well to fly it well. It is an exceptional machine that operates at the edge of the limitations of technology. It was designed in the 50s and will continue to operate through the decade. Flying at high speeds at low levels means that one small mistake and the plane will hit the ground before the pilot can realise that something has gone wrong. Though there are ways to recover and there is the option of ejecting, taking that split second decision is very hard.
In Kaddy's case though, it was the machine's fault. India is now in the process of phasing out MiG 21s. Kaddy's friends and family however will never truly recover from losing him. In the IAF though they're more accustomed than most to the possibility of death. The squadron raised a drink to Kaddy's memory that night and were back in their MiG 21 cockpits the next morning.

In conversation with Fighter Pilots #3

“Did you ever get scared?”

Danny “Never. It’s very rarely the planes’ fault, you know. It’s just that decisions have to be made in split seconds and people make small mistakes that cost them big.”

Roy “Sometimes, but never enough to stop doing it”

Singh “No, not really. Maybe a little. Occasionally accidents would happen but we’d drink on it and be back in the cockpit the next morning.”

Kanetkar “Well yes, but I think the fear is greater for the wives of fighter pilots. More than myself, It is them that I wonder about. I always wonder what it’s like for them when we leave every morning. I applaud them.”

07

A PUNNY STORY

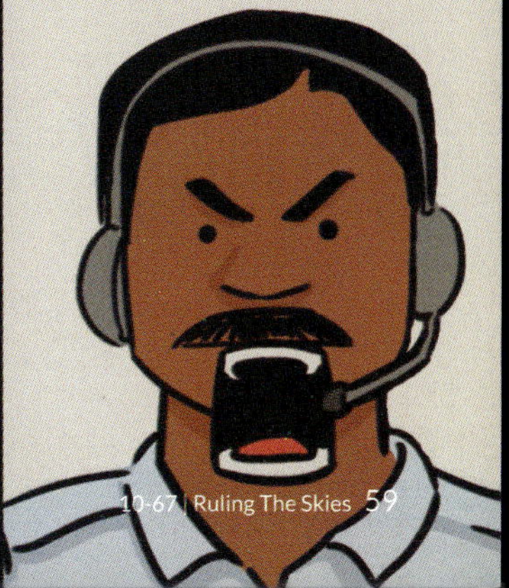

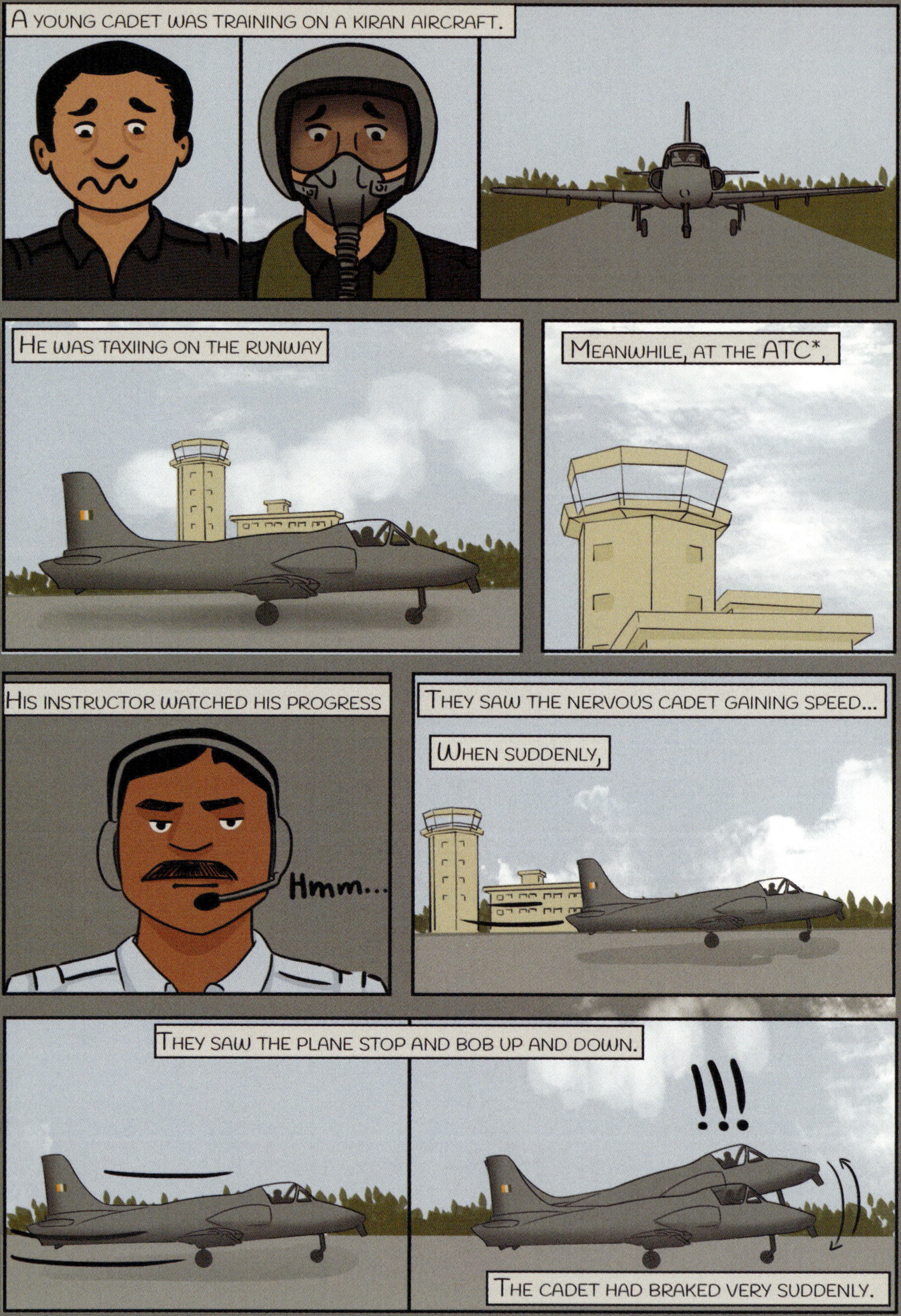

* AIR TRAFFIC CONTROL

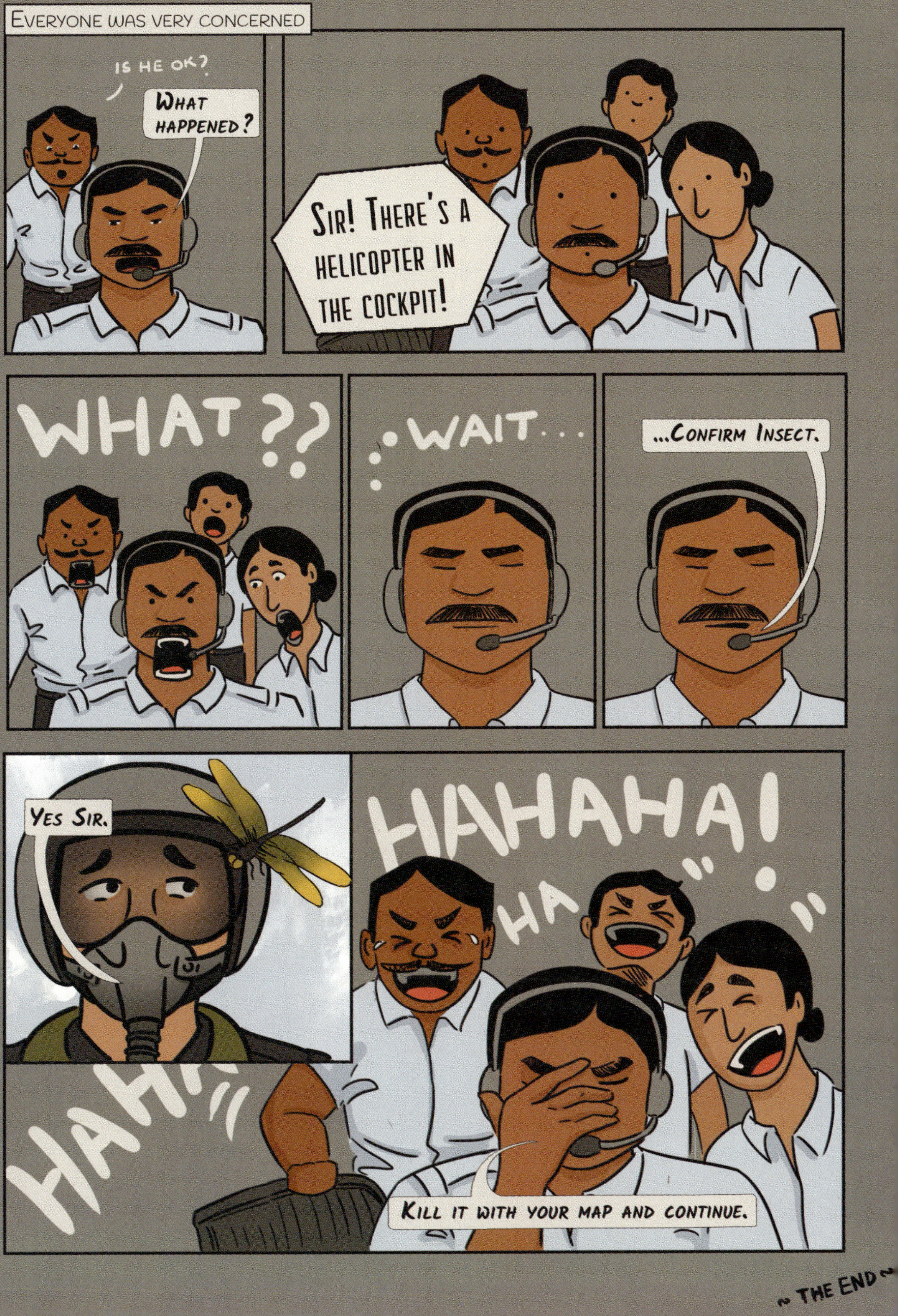
EVERYONE WAS VERY CONCERNED
IS HE OK?
WHAT HAPPENED?
SIR! THERE'S A HELICOPTER IN THE COCKPIT!
WHAT ??
WAIT...
...CONFIRM INSECT.
YES SIR.
HAHAHA!
HA
HAHA
KILL IT WITH YOUR MAP AND CONTINUE.
~ THE END ~

07

BEE-LIEVE IT OR NOT!

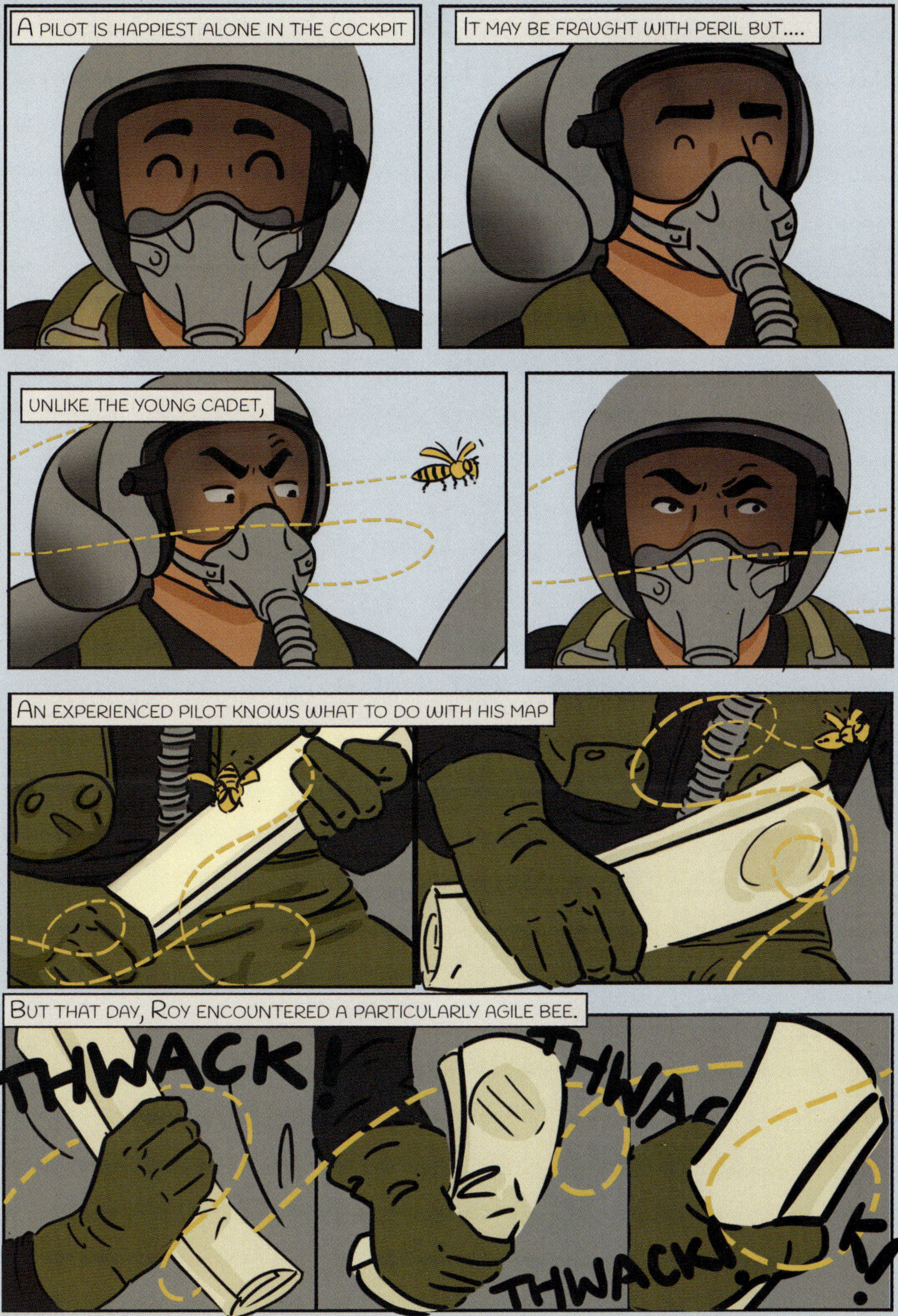
A PILOT IS HAPPIEST ALONE IN THE COCKPIT
IT MAY BE FRAUGHT WITH PERIL BUT....
UNLIKE THE YOUNG CADET,
AN EXPERIENCED PILOT KNOWS WHAT TO DO WITH HIS MAP
BUT THAT DAY, ROY ENCOUNTERED A PARTICULARLY AGILE BEE.
THWACK!
THWAC
THWACK!

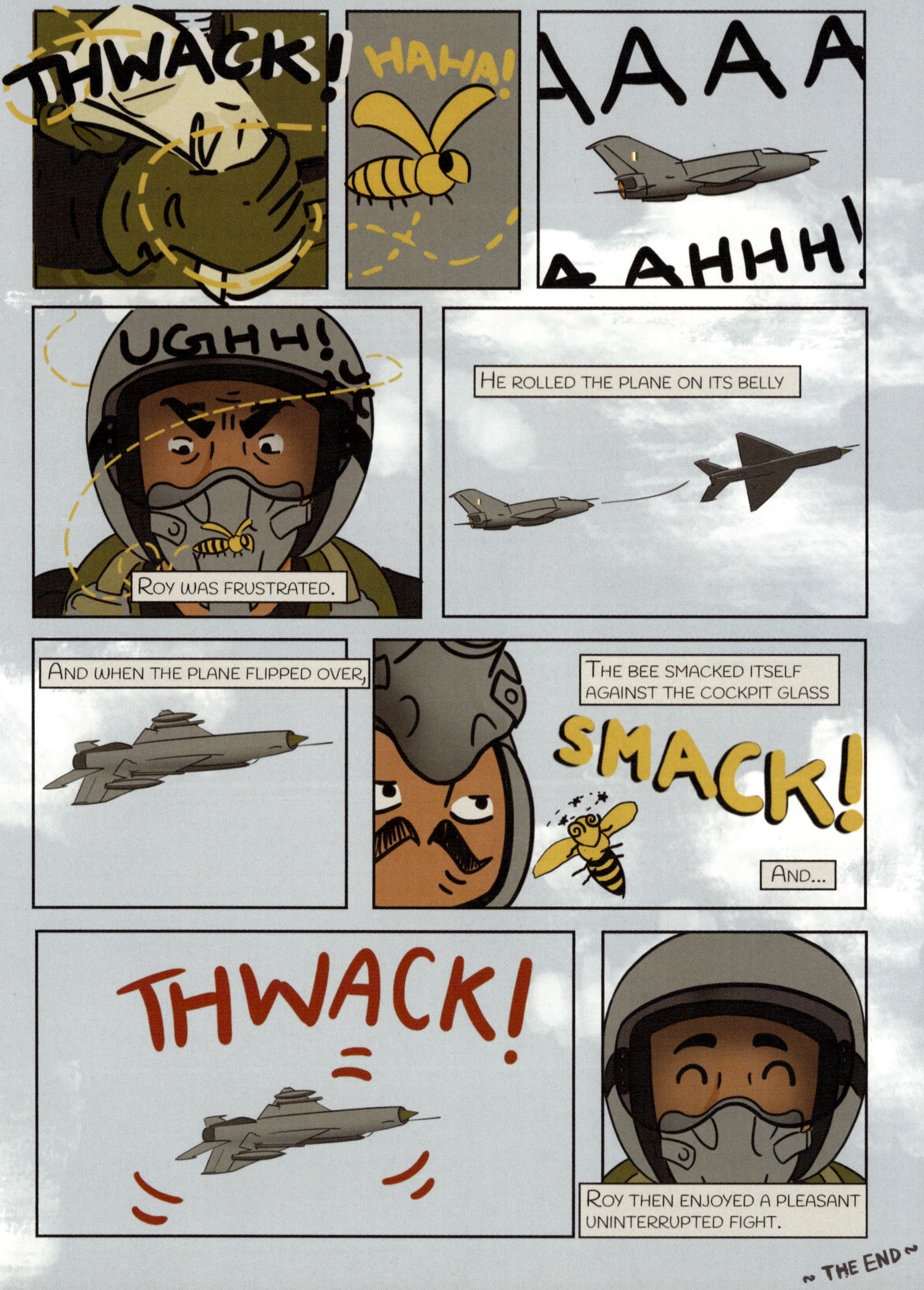
THWACK!
HAHA!
AAAA
AAHHH!
UGHH!
ROY WAS FRUSTRATED.
HE ROLLED THE PLANE ON ITS BELLY
AND WHEN THE PLANE FLIPPED OVER,
THE BEE SMACKED ITSELF AGAINST THE COCKPIT GLASS
SMACK!
AND...
THWACK!
ROY THEN ENJOYED A PLEASANT UNINTERRUPTED FIGHT.
~ THE END ~

09

HAATHI MISHRA

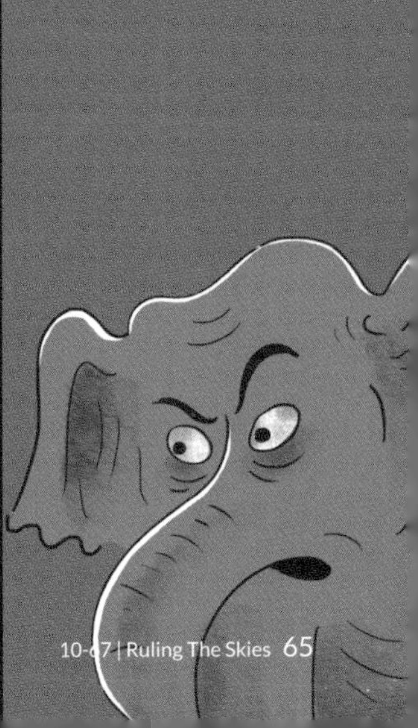

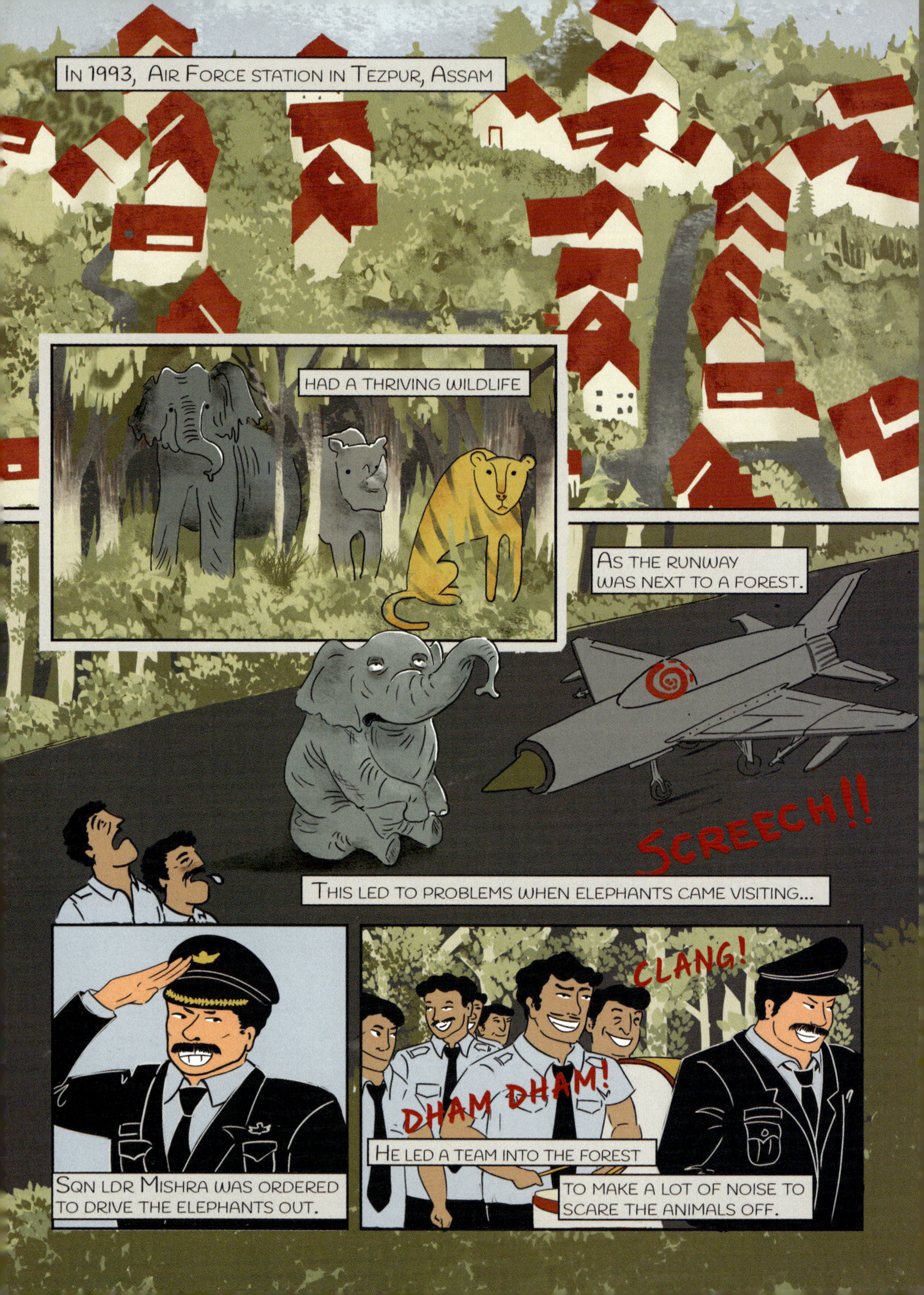

In 1993, Air Force station in Tezpur, Assam
had a thriving wildlife
As the runway was next to a forest.
SCREECH!!
This led to problems when elephants came visiting...
Sqn Ldr Mishra was ordered to drive the elephants out.
CLANG!
DHAM DHAM!
He led a team into the forest
to make a lot of noise to scare the animals off.

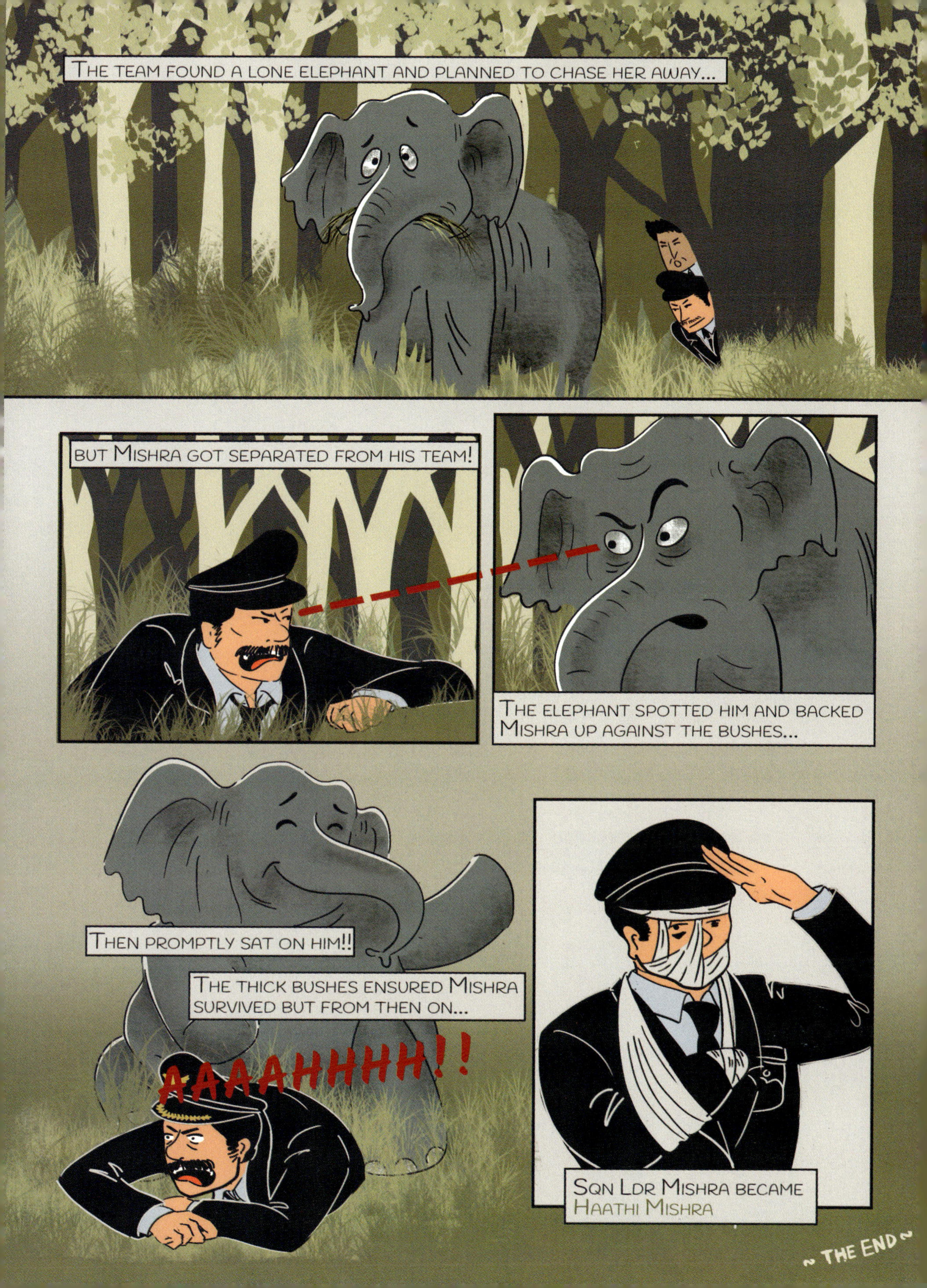

THE TEAM FOUND A LONE ELEPHANT AND PLANNED TO CHASE HER AWAY...
BUT MISHRA GOT SEPARATED FROM HIS TEAM!
THE ELEPHANT SPOTTED HIM AND BACKED MISHRA UP AGAINST THE BUSHES...
THEN PROMPTLY SAT ON HIM!!
THE THICK BUSHES ENSURED MISHRA SURVIVED BUT FROM THEN ON...
AAAAHHHHH!!
SQN LDR MISHRA BECAME HAATHI MISHRA
~ THE END ~

Tête-à-tête with Tony, IAF's Chief of Air Staff.

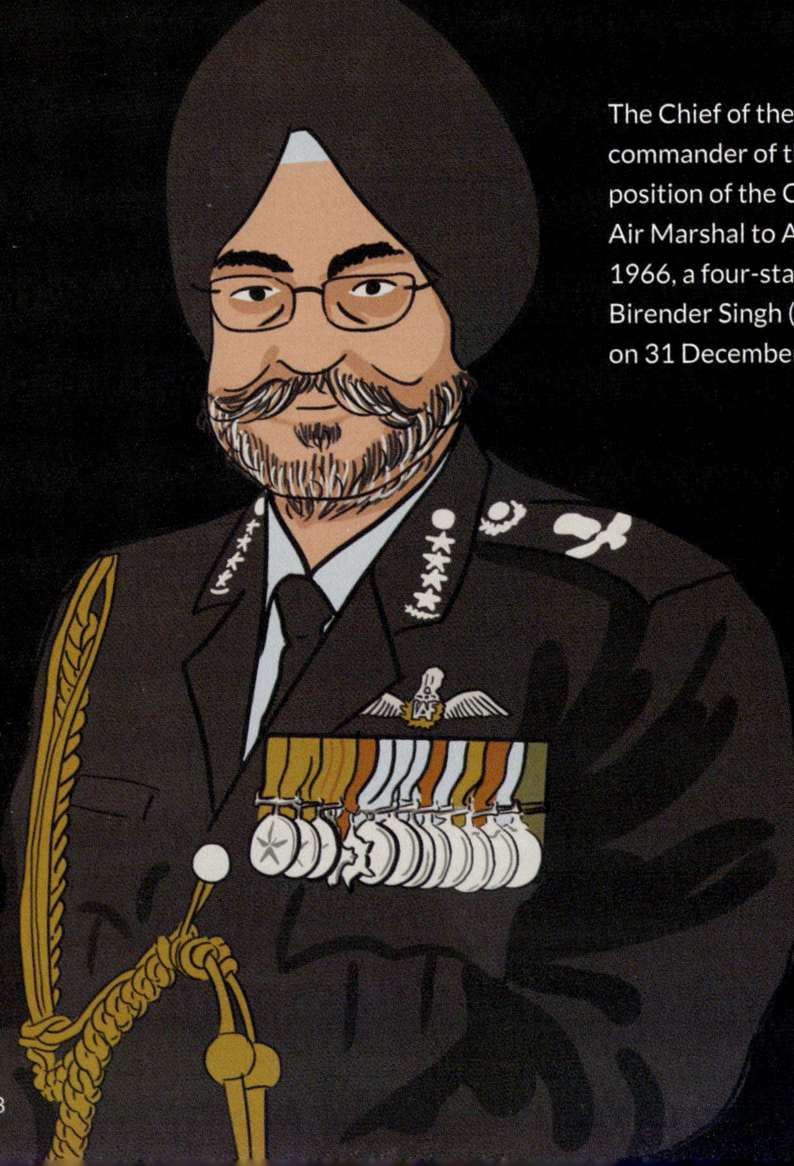

The Chief of the Air Staff (CAS)is the commander of the Indian Air Force. The position of the CAS was upgraded from Air Marshal to Air Chief Marshal in 1966, a four-star rank. Air Chief Marshal Birender Singh (Tony) Dhanoa took office on 31 December 2016 as the current CAS.

What made you want to join the Indian Air Force?

My grandfather was in the British Indian Army and he was deployed in Palestine in the First World War after which he was demobilized.
He went back to the village and completed his matriculation and then re-joined the Army and fought in the Second World War. He served in Singapore and later Egypt, where he went over a landmine and became a permanent CAT 'C' and could not be promoted beyond a Captain in the Army. He was deployed in the Kashmir Conflict as an Education Instructor and retired from Indian Army in 1950. Hence, he had led a very colorful life in the Army and regaled me with his stories as a young boy. He spent a lot of time with me during my school vacations.
My father joined the IAS as he couldn't join the Army due to his eyesight and over-qualification! He was an MA! My Uncle joined the IAF in 1965 as a Transport Pilot. Hence, I decided at a very early age to join the Military. At the age of 11, I appeared for an all India competition for RIMC (Rashtriya Indian Military College) and joined in Aug 1969. Subsequently as my very young uncle had just joined the Air Force, I decided I will join the Air Force.

What is the greatest thing about being a Fighter Pilot?

The greatest thing about being a fighter pilot is getting selected to become one. After passing out of NDA, plus some direct entry Cadets, we were 70 Cadets who joined the Elementary Flying School in Bidar, but only 35 got commissioned as Pilots, among them only 20 got Fighters, so 20 out of 70. The other good thing about being a Fighter pilot is that the Air Force is a skill based service, so you know how good you are and the rest of the world also knows how good you are. You don't have to prove anything to anyone, your performance is measurable. If your range scores are better than the other person, you are a better pilot. Simple!

You must have flown in some interesting terrain. What is the most beautiful thing you have seen while flying?

Normally while flying a single Cockpit Fighter, you don't have the time to appreciate the terrain. You have too many things to do. But since you asked this question, the answer is that during the Kargil War, we flew low level in the snow covered mountains on moonlit nights. The mountains were shining white, it was eerily beautiful as a lot of exchange of fire was taking place below us, we could see the tracers and the red hot butts of artillery shells. As late Flt Lt Dhariwal remarked, "Sir it seems as if they are trading cigarette butts with each other". Not exactly beautiful as you asked but once in a lifetime experience.

Was there an interesting training exercise you participated in? (eg. Some new planes that came in; Combat Exercises; a really fun sortie).

All training exercises are different but one interesting one was Dissimilar Air Combat Training (DACT) in our MiG-21 against the Naval Sea Harriers in Jamnagar in 1993-1994, where two of the Naval Pilots were those whom I had taught flying in the Air Force Academy. It was Guru Vs the Chela, an old aeroplane, the MiG-21 versus the newer Sea Harrier of the Indian Navy. Believe it or not we won most engagements as we were more experienced in Air Combat than the Navy.

"Air force is a close-knit family and we do remain friends forever. The best thing about NDA and the Military is that our best friends are seldom from my place or caste or community. It is the people with whom our ideas meet."

Air Force is a really close-knit community. Could you share a few stories about you and your friends' experiences?

Air force is a close-knit family and we do remain friends forever. The best thing about NDA and the Military is that our best friends are seldom from my place or caste or community. It is the people with whom our ideas meet. The Squadron Officers support the ladies who have unfortunately lost their husbands in flying accidents. One such case was a lady whom I knew as a bachelor. I used to bounce her house for meals. Her husband unfortunately died in a flying accident. She had two small children.
The Air Force ensured she got her pensionary benefits and she settled down in Pune. She took care of her two children and her old father-in-law. Whenever I visited Pune I looked her up and assisted her though she rarely asked for help. Now both her children are married and settled abroad. When the younger daughter got married and was going to Australia, I asked her "Who will look after you? You have sent both your children abroad." She instantaneously replied "Tony, You are there na!" It was the proudest moment for me.
I went all the way to 'Guntur' in Andhra Pradesh for my NDA course mate Koti Rao's son's wedding. We lost him in a MiG-21 accident in 1995-1996. The Squadron is a close-knit community. Recently a lady's husband died of a heart attack when he was flying for Air India after leaving the Air Force. She said the first people who reached her side were the Air Force Comrades of her late husband.

Fighter Jets are tricky and dangerous. Were there incidences that happened around you that were somewhat scary?

Fighter Jets are not tricky and dangerous but special skills are required to fly them. While most people do pass the driving test for cars, very few are selected for fighter operations. Compared to say the Hunter aircraft, the MiG-21 was less forgiving for the Russians had originally designed it as a high altitude, high speed Mach 2 (twice the speed of sound) Fighter/ Interceptor to mainly shoot down bombers threatening the then Soviet Union. We have used it for close combat, close air support, air interdiction and lastly as a lead in fighter trainer because the IAF did not have an Advance Jet Trainer (AJT) in the form of Hawks. So we had a number of accidents due to young pilots mishandling the aircraft transitioning from the Kiran at 200 Knots (360 Km) to MiG-21 at 600 Knots (1100 Km). Still we did manage to train a lot of pilots and reduce our accident rates during training.

You've flown a range of fighter planes, which one was your favourite and why? Do you ever miss flying fighters?

I have mainly flown the MiG-21 and Kiran aircraft with flying experience on other types in the back seat. So MiG-21 is my favorite as I have the maximum experience on it (~ 1800 Hours). I flew it as a Flight Commander, Commanding Officer and as a Station Commander. Flew solo as the Air Officer Commanding-In-Chief of South Western Air Command, Vice Chief of the Air Staff and as the Chief of the Air Staff. I loved the aircraft, it was much better than its contemporaries the

Mirage III and the Phantom F-4 in manoeuvrability. It does not have a very impressive combat record outside India mainly due to pilot's experience on the type. In 1971, the MiG-21s maintained 90% serviceability, their accurate bombing closed down both airfields in Dhaka effectively grounding the Pakistan Air Force in the East. In close combat, it got better of the F-104 Star Fighter and shot down two of them. It proved its versatility in Kargil, when with just a GPS as an additional aid to navigate, we used it for night bombing in the mountains.

Would you recommend joining the IAF as a fighter pilot to youngsters today? Why?

Yes, I would strongly recommend youngsters to join the Air Force for reasons that I have given in my answer to question No. 2.

> *"The greatest thing about being a fighter pilot is getting selected to become one... the Air Force is a skill based service, so you know how good you are and rest of the world also knows how good you are. You don't have to prove anything to anyone, your performance is measurable. If your range scores are better than the other person, you are a better pilot- SIMPLE!"*

Is there anything else you could share? Anything from the Air Force that is special to you?

A lot of people have asked me what has been my best moment in the Air Force? Was it when I became the Chief, the answer is no! It's when we win weapons meets, get declared as the best fighter squadron and after Kargil when we came out as the most decorated unit. It's like they say you are a "Tiger" & keep your shirt Top Button Open. Those are our most cherished moments!

I learnt that you had the chance to fly an MiG-21 again sometime back! How was the feeling of being inside the cockpit and in the skies again? Is flying like riding a bicycle or swimming?

I flew MiG-21 solo in 2015 (AOC-in-C, SWAC), 2016 (VCAS) and then 2017 as the CAS so I was in touch with flying the MiG-21. Before every such solo sortie, we practice our checks, procedures and emergencies on ground, fly a dual sortie in a trainer and then if the instructor clears you, go solo. Flying unlike swimming and cycling is a perishable skill.
You have to be current if you have to go solo. The aircraft is a machine it does not know who is inside (Flying Officer or an Air Marshal, Male or Female! It's Gender Neutral!). It follows the laws of physics so you have to be good to Aviate!

A little bit about Tony.

Air Chief Marshal Birender Singh Dhanoa aka Tony, took over as the Chief of the Air Staff on 01 January 2017. He was commissioned in 1978 as a fighter pilot. Tony has mainly flown the Kiran and MiG-21 aircraft but he has flying experience on the Jaguar, the MiG-29 & Su-30 MKI.

During the Kargil war, Tony was the Commanding Officer of a front line ground attack fighter squadron. He devised innovative methods of night bombing at high altitudes. This had never been tried before in the IAF. Post the conflict Tony's squadron emerged as the most decorated IAF unit of Kargil War. Tony holds the highest flying instructional category in the IAF and was handpicked to establish the 'IAF Training Team' abroad.

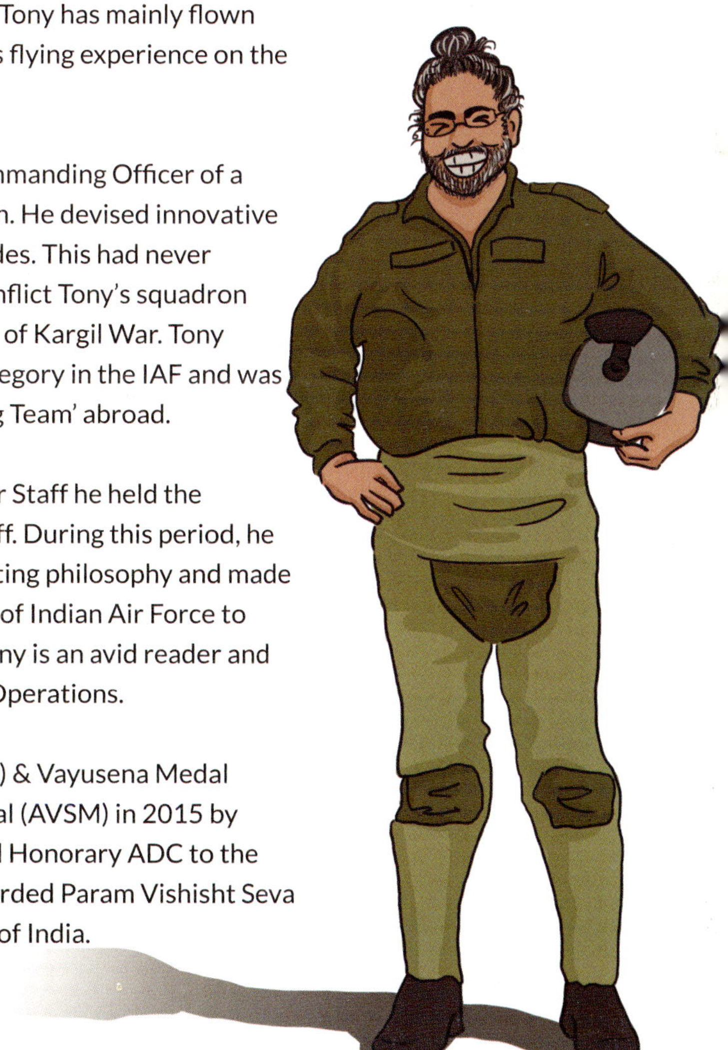

Before taking over as the Chief of the Air Staff he held the appointment of Vice Chief of the Air Staff. During this period, he developed a new concept of aerial targeting philosophy and made changes in the concept of air operations of Indian Air Force to contemporary war-fighting practices. Tony is an avid reader and writer on topics of Air Power and Joint Operations.

He was awarded Yudh Seva Medal (YSM) & Vayusena Medal (VM) in 1999 and Ati Vishisht Seva Medal (AVSM) in 2015 by the President of India. He was appointed Honorary ADC to the President of India on 01 Aug 15 and awarded Param Vishisht Seva Medal (PVSM) in 2016 by the President of India.

Combat Aircrafts in the Indian Air Force

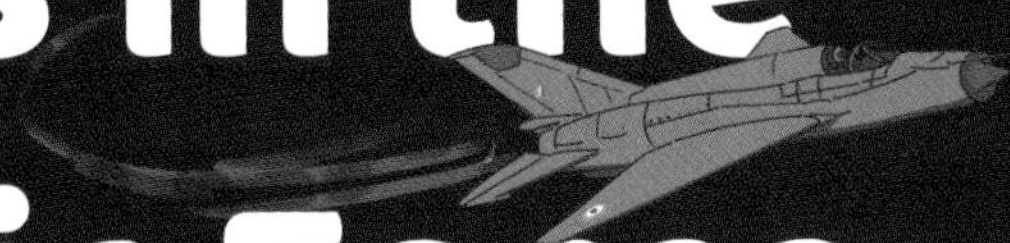

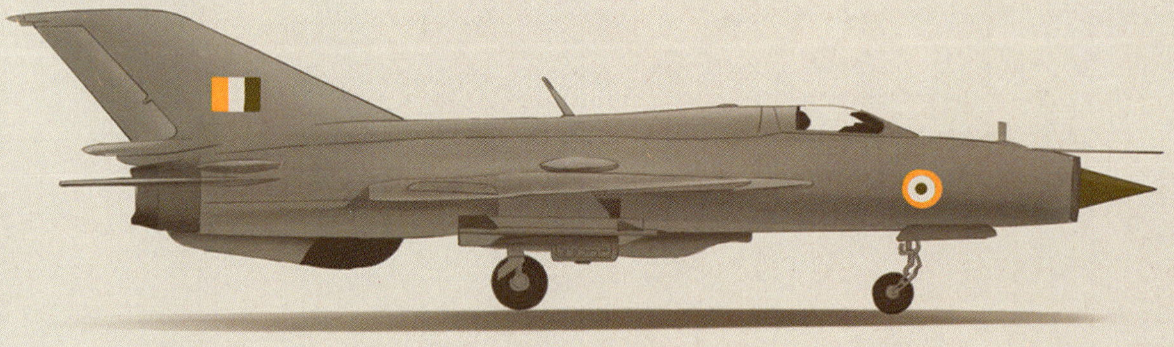

MIKOYAN-GUREVICH MiG-21

Role	Fighter and interceptor aircraft
National origin	Soviet Union
Maximum speed	Mach 2.0 (2,175 km/h, 1,351 mph)

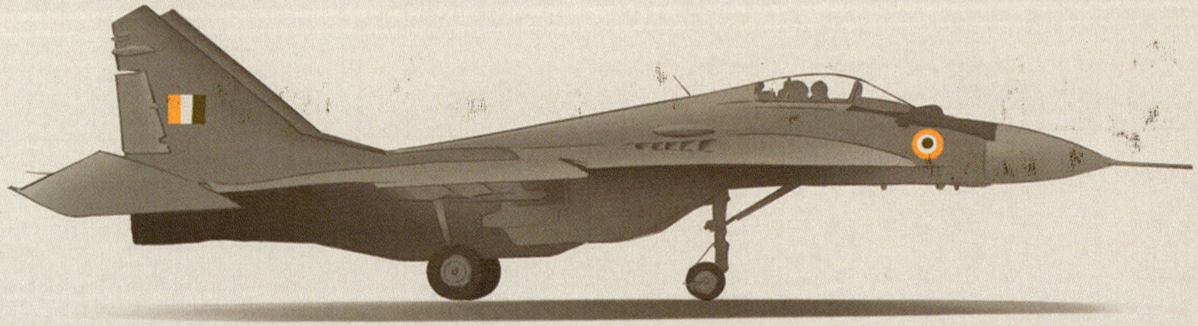

MIKOYAN MiG-29

Role	Air superiority fighter, multirole fighter
National origin	Soviet Union
Maximum speed	Mach 2.25 (2,400 km/h; 1,490 mph)

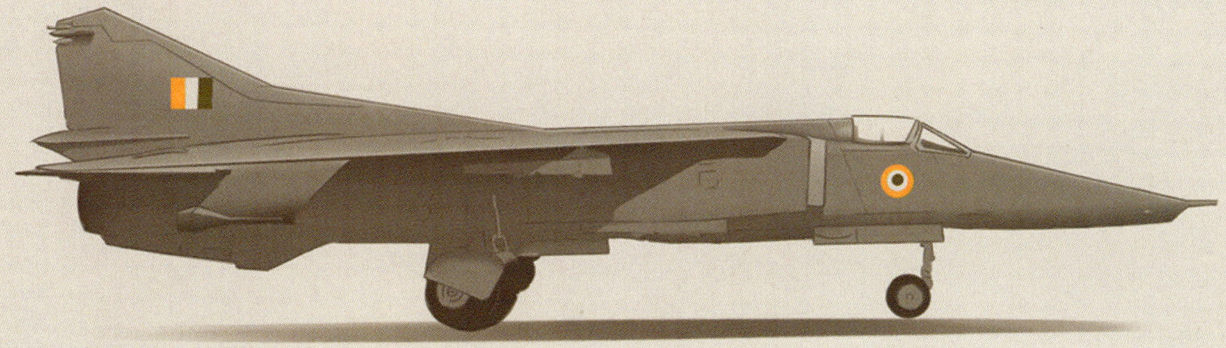

MIKOYAN MiG-27

Role	Ground-attack aircraft
National origin	Soviet Union
Maximum speed	Mach 1.5 (1,885 km/h; 1,171 mph)

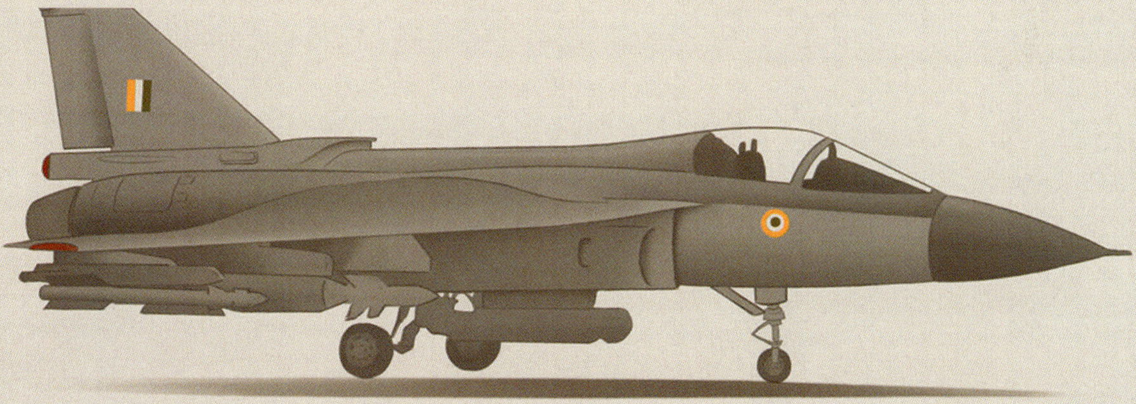

HAL TEJAS

Role	Multirole light fighter
National origin	India
Maximum speed	Mach 1.8 (2,205 km/h)

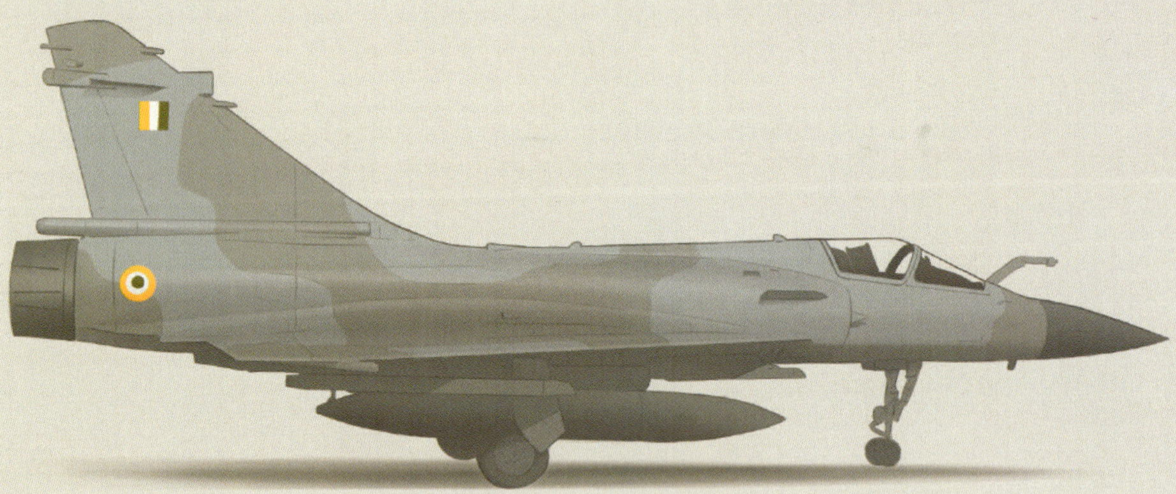

DASSAULT MIRAGE 2000

Role	Multirole fighter
National origin	France
Maximum speed	Mach 2.2 (2,336 km/h, 1,451 mph)

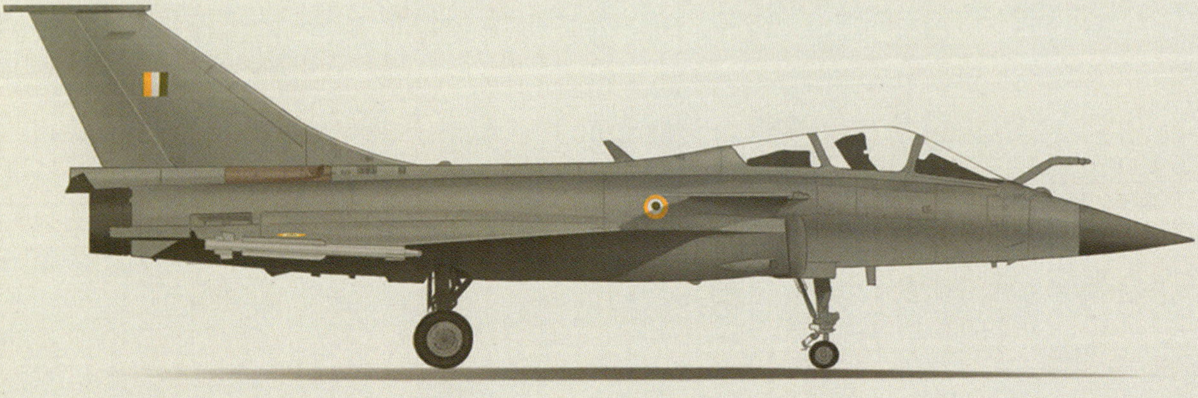

DASSAULT RAFALE

Role	Fighter and interceptor aircraft
National origin	France
Maximum speed	Mach 2.0 (2,175 km/h, 1,351 mph)

*Contracted. Yet to be inducted

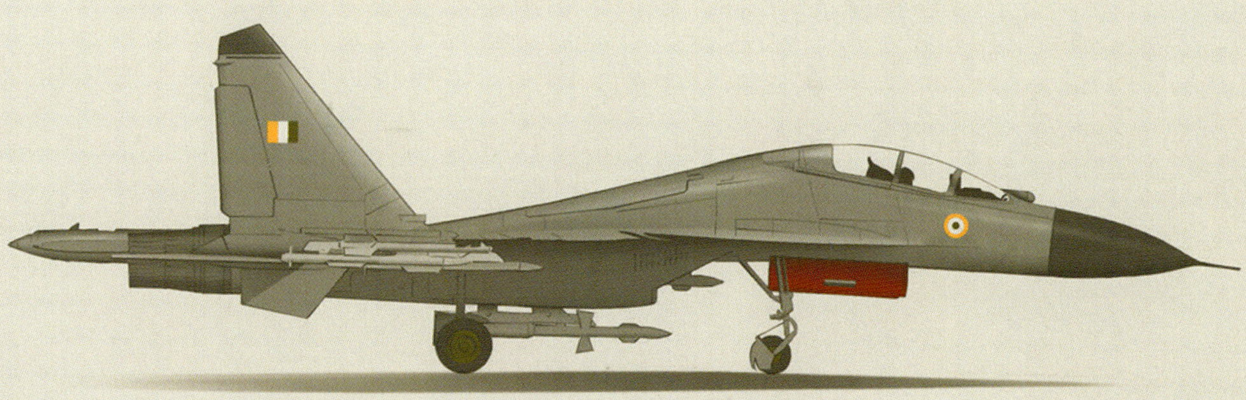

SUKHOI SU-30MKI

Role	Multirole air superiority fighter
National origin	Russia / India
Maximum speed	Mach 2 (2,120 km/h; 1,320 mi)

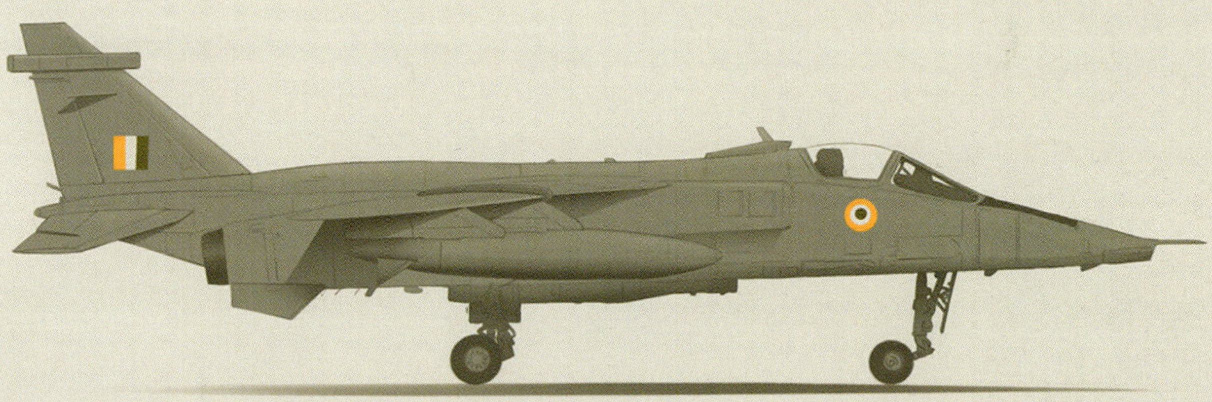

SEPECAT JAGUAR

Role	Attack aircraft
National origin	France/United Kingdom
Maximum speed	Mach 1.6 (1,699 km/h, 1,056 mph)

POSTFACE

"Flying might not be all plain sailing, but the fun of it is worth the price."

—Amelia Earhart,
The Fun of It, 1932

Fighter flying is a tough job, physically and emotionally. It demands its acolytes of their time and passion. Most fighter pilots shelve all their other interests and hobbies during their active fighter flying days because they simply do not have time to pursue any other passion. The typical day for a fighter pilot may start at dawn and continue till sunset. If there is a break in the afternoon then it is to allow a much needed siesta before the pilot is back for night flying. Yet, most fighter pilots love their jobs. They may decry their seniors, bad mouth the leadership but will never ever curse fighter flying which actually steals time and attention from all other activities.

Fighter flying can be challenging and unforgiving of mistakes. Every time a fighter pilot lights up his jet he knows he has the grim reaper as his passenger. It's like when James Bond said, "You only live twice. Once when you are born. And once when you look death in the face." At least six of the forty odd batch-mates that graduated with my father have ended up digging holes in the ground with a plane. That is more than one out of every ten. Those are horrifying odds and everyone of the pilots who shared their stories know this. Yet, almost all of them would jump at the chance of strapping on a fighter again if it was possible. Most pilots leave the Air Force after their active flying days are over. Of the many veterans I spoke to only two said they wouldn't want to fly a fighter again. I had this discussion with around fifty.

Fighter flying is not however only about adrenaline. It grants moments of great peace and beauty to its devotees. All fighter pilots will talk of moments, sometimes ordinary and sometimes extraordinary, that brought home the majesty of the Earth to them. Sometimes it is the glory of a snow clad Himalayan giant that looks broodingly down at them as they zip past it's shoulder at 20,000ft. Sometimes it's a precious sapphire blue tarn hidden like a jewel deep within the Kashmir valley. Sometimes it's that circular rainbow floating on a cloud. Tomorrow the sun and clouds will shift but the sight remains forever imprinted on the heart.

Two decades later my father still dreams and talks about the rice fields and the forests of Assam, lit bright green by the early morning sun as he made his way through puffy white cotton candy clouds. That is the joy, the beauty and privilege of fighter flying.

Oh! I have slipped the surly bonds of Earth
And danced the skies on laughter-silvered wings;
Sunward I've climbed, and joined the tumbling mirth
Of sun-split clouds, — and done a hundred things
You have not dreamed of — wheeled and soared and swung
High in the sunlit silence. Hov'ring there,
I've chased the shouting wind along, and flung
My eager craft through footless halls of air....

Up, up the long, delirious burning blue
I've topped the wind-swept heights with easy grace
Where never lark, or even eagle flew —
And, while with silent, lifting mind I've trod
The high untrespassed sanctity of space,
Put out my hand, and touched the face of God.

- John Gillespie Magee, Jr
Royal Canadian Air Force fighter pilot, WWII

GLOSSARY

Airfield
An open field designated for the taking off and landing by aircrafts. Unlike airports, airfields do not necessarily have terminals or paved runways.

ATC
Air traffic control. The ATC is a service provided by ground-based Air Traffic Controllers that direct flights, organize air traffic, prevent collisions and generally provide pilots with useful information.

Bogey
Unidentified aircraft suspected to be hostile.

Cadet
A trainee preparing to become an officer in the military.

CAP
Combat Air Patrol. Aircraft patrol provided over an area for intercepting and destroying hostile aircraft before they reach their target.

Cockpit
The flight deck from which a pilot controls the aircraft.

Cross Country
A flight between any two points that may not be on a defined air route.

Dissimilar Combat
Air combat training between different types of aircraft.

Dogleg

The Dog Leg Technique is a flight pattern to go around any navigational hazard.

The pilot turns away by 60° (say to the right) and starts the timer. After the hazard has been avoided, the pilot notes the time he flew away (say t seconds), steers back 120° left towards the original track and restarts the timer. When the time approaches t seconds he turns back to the right towards the original course and would now be on the original track.

Ejection

In the aircraft, an ejector seat is a system designed to rescue the pilot in an emergency. The seat is propelled out of the aircraft by an explosive charge, carrying the pilot with it.

Escort

Fighter aircraft designed to escort Bombers/ Strike aircraft to and from their targets.

Their job is to protect the Bomber/ Strike aircraft.

ETA

Estimated Time of Arrival.

G force

Gravitational force. A measurement of the type of acceleration that causes a perception of weight.

It is measured in g's, where 1 g is equal to the force of gravity at the Earth's surface. The g-force on an object is its acceleration relative to free-fall.

HAL

Hindustan Aeronautics Limited is an Indian state-owned aerospace and defence company.

It is involved in the design, fabrication and assembly of aircrafts, helicopters and their parts.

Mach

Mach number is a ratio of the speed of a body (aircraft) to the

speed of sound.
An aircraft is flying at Mach 1 if its speed is equal to the speed of sound in air. An aircraft flying at Mach 2 is flying at twice the speed of sound in air, etc.

Mph
Miles per hour. 1mph = 1.60934 km/h

Squadron
Field units and formations attached to static locations.
A flying squadron is a sub-unit of an air force station.
A fighter squadron in IAF generally consists of 18 aircraft.

Squadron Diaries
Large horizontal format diaries written in and maintained by the fighter pilots of every squadron. These diaries include details of flying and activities unrelated to flying in the squadron like social occasions, family life etc. These are shared diaries of the pilots (but usually filled in by one person with good hand writing) and span decades.

NDA
National Defence Academy. Joint Services academy of the Indian Armed Forces, where cadets of the three services, the Army, the Navy and the Air Force train together before they go on to respective Service Academies for further pre-commissioning training.
It is the first tri-service academy in the world.

PFL
Practice Forced Landing. Training scenario to help pilots develop sufficient skills to cope with an emergency situations.
For example, when the pilot if forced to carry out a landing following an engine failure.

Reheat
An afterburner (or a reheat) is a component present on some jet engines, mostly those used on military supersonic aircraft.

Its purpose is to provide an increase in thrust, usually for supersonic flight, takeoff, and combat situations.

RT
Radio Transmission.

Sqn Ldr
Squadron Leader. A rank of officer in the IAF, above Flight Lieutenant and below Wing Commander.

Strike
A role in which the fighter aircraft carries an air-to-ground attack.

Taxiing
The process of the aircraft moving slowly on the ground before take-off or after landing.

Wg Cdr
Wing Commander. A commissioned rank in the IAF. It ranks immediately above Squadron Leader and below Group Captain.